THE SEVEN
WILLIAM SHA

The Best of the Bard for Beginners
An anthology chosen by David Hughes

en Press

First published in Great Britain by Pen Press

All paper used in the printing of this book has been made from wood grown in man-
aged, sustainable forests.

ISBN13: 978-1-907499-69-2

Printed and bound in the UK
Pen Press is an imprint of Indepenpress Publishing Limited
25 Eastern Place
Brighton
BN2 1GJ

A catalogue record of this book is available from
the British Library

Cover design by Jacqueline Abromeit

To the memory of my father, John Armstrong Hughes (1876-1942) Shakespeare actor, producer, lecturer and broadcaster.

This book would not have been possible without the patient labour of my daughter Tanya Hughes, who spent many hours transcribing the complex type script onto the computer.

◊   ◊   ◊

Not marble, nor the gilded monuments
Of princes, shall outlive this powerful rhyme;
But you shall shine more bright in these conténts
Than unswept stone, besmeared with sluttish time.
When wasteful war shall statues overturn,
And broils root out the work of masonry,
Nor Mars his sword nor war's quick fire shall burn
The living record of your memory.
'Gainst death and all-oblivious enmity
Shall you pace forth; your praise shall still find room
Even in the eyes of all posterity
That wears this world out to the ending doom.   (Sonnet 55)

◊   ◊   ◊

_____

Contents

The text is based on that of the Arden Shakespeare.
Where early editions have variant readings,
F stands for that found in the First Folio of 1623,
Q signifies a reading found in one of the Quartos.

Line references are approximate.

INTRODUCTION

THE SEVEN AGES OF WILLIAM SHAKESPEARE
The Best of the Bard for Beginners

It is a truism that every new generation has to find its own way of coping with the chances and changes of life, in the course of which we make many mistakes, commit sins and follies, and frequently find ourselves in painful and sometimes harrowing situations. Most of us have experienced disappointments and frustrations in the course of our careers. We have sometimes acted stupidly, but are always hoping to find the key to a balanced and satisfying life, a rule to live by, and answers to human dilemmas. All who think at all are still looking for that elixir of life, that utopia, that rock of certainty where all our anxieties may melt away. As we mature we begin to realise that there is no such simple key to life, no one answer, but we are glad to welcome any crumbs of wisdom as we happen to stumble upon them. Some have found comfort in religion, some in psychoanalysis, some in political activity, some in the caring professions, some in yoga, some in crude hedonism. For me, comfort is to be found in the writings of William Shakespeare. The plays of Shakespeare portray human nature in all its variety, from self-sacrificing heroism to the very depths of savage barbarism, from love to jealous hate, from generosity to ingratitude, from openness to hypocrisy, from the infliction of cruelty to remorse and redemption.

The aim of this book is to use the enormous volume of Shakespeare's writing as a quarry from which to extract a coherent philosophy of life, to guide us between the cradle and the grave. Some will object that we must view each play as a whole, in order to absorb its message, and not chop it up for the sake of finding aphorisms and moral maxims. Others will say that the speeches which Shakespeare puts into the mouths of his characters do not necessarily reflect his own outlook on life. In such cases the reader will use his own judgment to distinguish the true insight from the false.

A further objection will be put forward that we cannot find reality in plays written hastily four centuries ago, in archaic language, with far-fetched plots, and characters who are mere puppets contrived to fit those plots. To answer that, I must call upon witnesses whose judgment will be universally respected.

1

Firstly, William Hazlitt:

> Shakespeare does not present us with groups of stage-puppets or poetical machines making set speeches on human life, and acting from a calculation of ostensible motives, but he brings living men and women on the scene, who speak and act from real feelings, according to the ebbs and flows of passion.

(Characters of Shakespeare's plays, 1817)

And here is Hazlitt on the character of Hamlet:

> This is that Hamlet the Dane ... all whose thoughts we seem to know as well as we do our own ... Hamlet is a name; his speeches and sayings but the idle coinage of the poet's brain. What then, are they not real? They are as real as our own thoughts. Their reality is in the reader's mind. It is *we* who are Hamlet.

His testimony is echoed by that of John Dryden:

> ... Shakespeare was the man of all Modern, and perhaps Ancient Poets, had the largest and most comprehensive soul ... When he describes anything, you more than see it, you feel it too ... He needed not the spectacle of Books to read Nature; he look'd inwards, and found her there. ... he is always great, when some great occasion is presented to him.

(From Of Dramatick Poesie, An Essay, 1668)

And in his preface to Troilus and Cressida (1679):

> Shakespear had an Universal mind, which comprehended all Characters and Passions.

Alexander Pope added his voice to the general consensus:

> If ever any Author deserved the name of an Original, it was Shakespear. ...Every single character in Shakespear is as much an Individual, as those in Life itself; it is . . impossible to find any two alike. ... he is not more a master of the Great, than of the Ridiculous in human nature; of our noblest tendernesses than of our vainest foibles ... He seems to have known the world by Intuition, to have look'd *thro'* humane nature at one glance.

(Preface to Works of Shakespear, 1725)

In the following century we have the judgment of Victor Hugo:

> What is he? You might almost answer, He is the earth
> ... the globe ... existence ... In Shakespeare the birds sing, the
> rushes are clothed with green, hearts love, souls suffer, the cloud
> wanders, it is hot, it is cold, night falls, time passes, forests and
> multitudes speak, the vast eternal dream hovers over all. Sap and
> blood, all forms of the multiple reality, actions and ideas, man
> and humanity, the living and the life, solitudes, cities, religions,
> diamonds and pearls, dunghills and charnel-houses, the ebb and
> flow of beings, the steps of comers and goers, all, all are on Shake-
> speare and in Shakespeare; and, this genius being the earth, the
> dead emerge from it ...
>
> (William Shakespeare, 1864)

In our own day Harold Blum has written:

> No Western writer, or any Eastern author I am able to read, is equal
> to Shakespeare as an intellect, and among writers I would include the
> principal philosophers, the religious sages, and the psychologists from
> Montaigne through Nietsche to Freud.
>
> (Shakespeare, the Invention of the Human, pp 1-2)

One explanation of his universality is that he wrote the plays for a wide
range of spectators. The various companies of players were only able to
exist and flourish under the patronage and protection of prominent persons such as the Lord Chamberlain, the Lord Admiral, the Earl of Leicester, the Earl of Pembroke and the Earl of Derby. The performances had to
appeal therefore to people of education and courtly manners, and on so
many occasions were played before royalty. Ben Jonson, in his Preface to
the First Folio of Shakespeare's collected works (1623), referred to

> those flights upon the bankes of Thames
> That did so take Eliza, and our James!

By contrast, the floor of the theatre, the pit, provided standing room
for a penny, and Shakespeare, in the famous scene where Hamlet gives
acting advice to the players, makes a disparaging comment on the gross-
er manners of the spectators in the pit:

> O, it offends me to the soul to hear a robustious periwig-
> pated fellow tear a passion to tatters, to very rags, to split the ears
> of the groundlings, who for the most part are capable of nothing
> but inexplicable dumbshows and noise. (3.2.8)

3

Ben Jonson in a preface to a friend's play, listed the various characters who would be found in a typical audience: gamester, captain, knight, knight's servant, lady, woman of doubtful reputation, shop's foreman, brave sparks. A century later, Alexander Pope guessed that Shakespeare's audiences had been "generally composed of the meaner sort of people; and therefore the Images of Life were to be drawn from those of their own rank; accordingly we find that not only our Author's only but almost all the old Comedies have their scene among Tradesmen and Mechanicks ..."

(Preface to The Works of Shakespear, 1725)

The fact that audiences included a variety of rogues, prostitutes and pickpockets was a principal reason why the Puritans, who controlled London and much of England in the 1640s, closed down all theatres, and finally dismantled them after 1644.

William Shakespeare was an actor before he was a playwright, and in that profession he learned to enter into the minds of many characters and to portray them with conviction. Hamlet tells the players "the purpose of playing ... was and is to hold as 'twere the mirror up to nature; to show virtue her own feature, scorn her own image, and the very age and body of the time his form and pressure" (Ham 3.2.24) (That last word means impress or stamp.) The experience of acting would have given him the perceptiveness to know, when he turned to writing plays, what words and situations would best draw out a response from the audience.

It would follow from his upbringing in Stratford upon Avon that he would be able to recreate in his plays the characters he saw about him in the daily life of street or market. But his genius also enabled him to delineate convincingly the life of the educated classes, the life of the nobility and even of royalty itself. Where did he gain the experience to paint in words these confident portraits? Some of this he could have based on an imaginative use of the description of those classes derived from his school study of the classics and his reading of English history. For example in writing Antony and Cleopatra he closely follows Plutarch[*]

(North's Plutarch, describing Cleopatra :)

> (she took) her barge in the river of Cydnus, the poop whereof
> was of gold, the sails of purple, and the oars of silver, which kept

---

[*]   Plutarch's Lives: Sir Thomas North's translation, printed 1579, 1595. See pp 91-
       94, 117 for further examples

stroke in rowing after the sound of the music of flutes … And now for the person of herself: she was laid under a pavilion of cloth of gold of tissue, apparelled and attired like the goddess Venus, commonly drawn in picture: and hard by her, on either hand of her, pretty fair boys apparelled as painters do set forth god Cupid. with little fans in their hands…

(Shakespeare:)

> The barge she sat in, like a burnish'd throne,
> Burned on the water: the poop was beaten gold;
> Purple the sails, and so perfumed that
> The winds were love-sick with them; the oars were silver,
> Which to the tune of flutes kept stroke.
>   … For her own person,
> It beggared all description: she did lie
> In her pavilion–cloth of gold of tissue –
> O'er-picturing that Venus where we see
> The fancy outwork nature; on each side her
> Stood pretty dimpled boys, like smiling Cupids,
> With divers-coloured fans…   (2.2.192)

And in the plays based on British history it is very apparent that he is following closely the accounts given in Raphael Holinshed's Chronicles of England, Scotland and Ireland (1577), and Edward Hall's Chronicle (1548).

Of course, these sources were not unbiased histories in the modern sense, and we should not look for historical accuracy in the plays, which were written to provide a brief entertainment. Shakespeare often takes a historical figure, and then attaches to him or her an imagined personality, placing them in situations of his own creation to see how they might behave. The real Macbeth, Richard IIIrd, Henry Vth, Antony and so forth had characters significantly different from those portrayed in the plays, which nevertheless remain penetrating studies of human behaviour.

Ben Jonson, in that preface to the first complete edition of the plays, rates Shakespeare, as a dramatist, higher than "all that insolent Greece or haughty Rome sent forth" despite having "small Latin and less Greek," implying that his education had been perfunctory and superficial. Although there is no documentary proof that Shakespeare attended the grammar school at Stratford, it is unthinkable that, as the son of a leading citizen and alderman of the town he did not do so. The Latin lesson in the Merry Wives of Windsor is based upon the standard School text-book of the grammar schools of that period. In such schools the authors studied would have included Erasmus, Ovid, Terence, Sallust and Virgil. Among the exercises Shakespeare would have had to undertake would have been passages of Latin prose turned into Latin verse. In addition he would be required to prepare and deliver orations based upon the principles of logical argument. All this would have been supervised by Oxford-educated masters during Shakespeare's time there, Simon Hunt (1571-5), Thomas Jenkins (1571-9) and John Cottom (1579-81).

Why did such an intelligent young man not to go on to university after his schooldays? Probably the reason was lack of money. His father, John Shakespeare, began to get into financial difficulties in 1578, when he was obliged to mortgage property in order to raise money, which he was unable to pay back in 1580, when William was sixteen, a customary age for entry to the university. Even if he had gone there, we may guess that his quick mind would have been stifled by the over-formal atmosphere of the instruction, judging from a passage in one of his early plays, Love's Labour's Lost:

> (Berowne asks:) What is the end of study? let me know.
> (Ferdinand, King of Navarre:)
> Why, that to know which else we should not know.
> (Berowne:)
> Things hid and barred, you mean, from common sense?
> ... all delights are vain; but that most vain
> Which, with pain purchased doth inherit pain:
> As, painfully to pore upon a book,
> To seek the light of truth; while truth the while
> Doth falsely blind the eyesight of his look.
>
> ... ...
> Study is like the heaven's glorious sun,
> That will not be deep-searched with saucy looks;
> Small have continual plodders ever won,
> Save base authority from others' books.
> These earthly godfathers of heaven's lights
> That give a name to every fixèd star,
> Have no more profit of their shining nights
> Than those that walk and wot not they are. (1.1.55)

Unforeseen events would in any case have directed him away from university, and towards the necessity of earning a living. In 1582, when Shakespeare was 18, he married Anne Hathaway, who was 26, and pregnant with their first child, Susanna, born in May of the following year. After a record of the baptism of his twin children Hamnet and Judith in 1585 there is no document mentioning him until 1592, when he was well established on the London theatrical scene. Thus from his marriage to 1592 there is a ten-year gap in what we know of his life, and there have been many guesses which attempt to suggest what he was doing during that time.

The antiquary John Aubrey (1626-97) compiled materials for short biographies of prominent people of that age, later edited and published under the title Brief Lives. In Shakespeare's case he must have carried out some of his research in Stratford, for he writes: "I have been told by some of the neighbours..."   so we may give some credence to his information. In a letter he wrote: "Did I tell you that I have met with old Mr Beeston who knew all the old English poets, whose lives I am taking from him: his father was Master of the Playhouse." The latter was Christopher Beeston, an actor and colleague of Shakespeare's in the Lord Chamberlain's Company of players. William Beeston, the son, told Aubrey that Shakespeare "understood Latin pretty well, for he had been in his younger yeares a schoolmaster in the countrey." That has been taken to mean that he had acted as tutor in the household of a gentleman or nobleman. If that is true, then it explains how he might have seen at first hand the manners and conversation of the 'upper classes.' It is tempting to speculate that the head of the household was one of those justices so comprehensively ridiculed in Henry IV (part 2). For further clues about the lost years, see the note at the end of the chapter.

William would have seen good acting from an early age. His father, John Shakespeare, as Borough Chamberlain for Stratford, paid for visits of the Queen's Players in 1568, and the Earl of Worcester's in 1569. Acting companies came again in 1573, 1575, 1576, and at least once a year after 1579. William must have attended, and was probably as thrilled as was his exact contemporary, R. Willis of Gloucester, who wrote:

> "If the Mayor like the actors... he appoints them to play before himself and the aldermen... At such a play my father took me and made me stand between his legs as he sat upon one of the benches where we saw and heard very well ... This sight took

such impression in me that when I came towards man's estate it was as fresh in my memory as if I had seen it newly acted."

(Mount Tabor, 1639)

How did Shakespeare move into the world of the theatre? In the year 1587 no fewer than five companies of players performed in Stratford, including the Earl of Leicester's Company and the Queen's Men. Both companies were short of players. In the case of the Queen's Men, one of their actors, William Knell, had just been killed in a brawl, so they would have needed to recruit a replacement without delay. This was an opportunity which the 23-year-old Shakespeare might have seized, conscious that he had the passion for language which would fit him for such a profession.

> There is a tide in the affairs of men,
> Which, taken at the flood, leads on to fortune;
> Omitted, all the voyage of their life
> Is bound in shallows and in miseries.
> On such a full sea are we now afloat,
> And we must take the current when it serves,
> Or lose our ventures.

(JC 4.3.217)

Experience of the stage would not have been essential: novices would learn as they went along. The great actor Edward Alleyn joined the Earl of Worcester's Men at the age of sixteen.

As soon as the young Shakespeare arrived in London he would have found himself surrounded by an enormous range of characters, material to be studied, and worked into his plays in due course. Thomas Dekker gives a vivid picture of the inhabitants of London in 1606, writing that the streets echoed with the cries of hawkers, and touts seeking customers for shops: "What do you lack? Do you buy, sir? See what you lack? Pins, points, garters, Spanish gloves, silk ribbons. Crabs! Pears! Shoes! Small coal! Writing ink!" A set of woodcuts showing more street cries includes: 'chimney-sweep', 'hott pudding-pyes hott', 'fine Sevil oranges', 'who buys my fine sausage', 'buy a matt for a bed' and 'my rope of onions.'

William Harrison, in his Description of England (1587) lists some of the "rogues and idle persons" to be found "such as gad about the country": "practisers of physiognomy and palmistry, tellers of fortune, fencers, players, minstrels, jugglers, pedlars, tinkers, pretended scholars". In the 1580s one John Hawes raised the question:

Why do the streets yet swarm with beggars, that no man can stand or stay in any church or street but presently 10 or 12 beggars come breathing in his face, many of them having their plague sores and other contagious diseases running on them?

And a letter from the Lord Major of London to the Privy Council (1597) complained that the theatres themselves attracted "vagrant persons, masterless men, thieves, horse stealers, whoremongers, cozeners, coney-catchers, contrivers of treason and other idle and dangerous persons ... " Plenty of variety here then to provide material for Shakespeare's pen.

In 1623, seven years after Shakespeare's death, his fellow actors John Heminge and Henry Condell, edited the first printed edition of his collected plays, the so-called First Folio. They wrote that their motive was "only to keep the memory of so worthy a friend and fellow alive as was our Shakespeare." They addressed the book "to the great variety of readers, from the most able, to him that can but spell," and they urged "whatever you do, buy." They went on: "read him, therefore; and again and again: and if then you do not like him, surely you are in some manifest danger, not to understand him."

It is not enough to have heard Shakespeare praised to the skies and hailed as a genius, but you, the reader, should set those appraisals aside, and make your own judgement as you read his work. And if you are to understand him, you will have to bring your own imagination into play, as Shakespeare himself pleaded in the Prologue to Henry Vth:

Let us ...
... on your imaginary forces work ...
Piece out our imperfections with your thoughts ...
Think, when we talk of horses, that you see them
Printing their proud hoofs i' th' receiving earth;
For 'tis your thoughts that now must deck our kings,
Carry them here and there, jumping o'er times
Turning th' accomplishment of many years
Into an hourglass ...   (Prol. 17)

The appeal to the imagination of readers and audience continues in the Chorus which introduces Act 3:

Thus with imagined wing our swift scene flies
In motion of no less celerity
Than that of thought. Suppose that you have seen

The well-appointed King at Hampton pier   (Southampton)
Embark his royalty; and his brave fleet
With silken streamers the young Phoebus fanning.   (the rising sun)
Play with your fancies, and in them behold
Upon the hempen tackle shipboys climbing;
Hear the shrill whistle which doth order give
To sounds confused ...
                              Follow, follow!
Grapple your minds to sternage of this navy,
And leave your England ...
Work, work your thoughts, and therein see a siege ...   (Harfleur)
...   Still be kind
And eke out our performance with your mind.   (Chorus, 3)

The audience at a Shakespeare play know that the words are "but the idle coinage of the poet's brain", yet the very fact that they choose to attend the theatre acknowledges that they are prepared to suspend disbelief and accept the 'reality' of the stage action, and are willing to have their emotions engaged and swayed, by empathy with the lovers, revulsion against the murderers, indignation at the deviousness of the hypocrites and traitors, and moved to laughter with the clowns and wits. We hope that at the end the lovelorn will get together, the misunderstandings will be solved, and the villains will get their come-uppance. In the same way that an audience thus enters into the spirit of a play, the reader must make his own contribution by exerting his imagination, and thereby actively seeking the meaning behind Shakespeare's words. And over and beyond that meaning is the poetry, the rich sounds of the words and the rhythm that carries them along. To appreciate that, it is worth rolling the phrases round the tongue a few times. At random I offer these examples:

How silver-sweet sound lovers' tongues by night,
Like softest music to attending ears!   (R&J 2.2.165)

. ...
                    the innocent sleep:
Sleep that knits up the ravell'd sleeve of care,
The death of each day's life, sore labour's bath,
Balm of hurt minds, great nature's second course,
Chief nourisher in life's feast.   (Mac 2.2.37)

. ...
                    Say to Athens,
Timon hath made his everlasting mansion   (his grave)

10

Upon the beached verge of the salt flood,
Who once a day with his embossed froth
The turbulent surge shall cover.   (TA 5.1.219)
(Note how the word-sounds echo the sound of the sea)

                    ... ...

Writers in the Elizabethan age were able to use the English language in a remarkably free and fluid way. The language had not yet been circumscribed and confined by grammars, dictionaries and pedants. Many new words were being borrowed from French and Italian. As Ivor Brown put it, in a happy expression, "To the good ale of Chaucerian English had been added the wine of the Renaissance."   (Shakespeare, p 333)

Shakespeare was therefore able to adapt the language to his purpose without inhibition, and indeed he is credited with introducing some two thousand new words, now in everyday use, such as: accommodation, barefaced, countless, courtship, dextrous, dislocate, eventful, excellent, horrid, indistinguishable, premeditated, reliance, temporary, untie, unvarnished, vast. In addition he coined many useful hybrids, such as ill-tuned, leap-frog, lack-lustre, sea-change, and smooth-faced. His extraordinary memory was able to draw on a vocabulary of over 21,000 words, more than three times the number used in the Old Testament. One may say that this free use of language and lack of inhibition was a major reason for his pre-eminence as a writer, so that, as his friends the editors of the First Folio said of him: "his mind and hand went together. And what he thought he uttered with that easiness, that we have scarce received from him a blot in his papers." (i.e.corrections)

Hazlitt puts his finger on the secret of Shakespeare's genius as a dramatist:

> "Each of his characters is as much itself, and as absolutely independent of the rest, as well as of the author, as if they were living persons, not fictions of the mind. ... By an art like that of the ventriloquist, he throws his imagination out of himself, and makes every word appear to proceed from the mouth of the person in whose name it is given ... His characters are real beings of flesh and blood; they speak like men, not like authors. One might suppose that he had stood by at the time and overheard what had passed... The dialogues in Shakespeare are carried on without any consciousness of what is to follow, without any appearance of preparation or premeditation. The gusts of passion come and go like sounds of music borne on the wind."

(From Lectures on the English Poets, 1818)

Shakespeare stands supreme as a dissector of human nature, because he portrays us as most of us really are, namely a mixture of virtuous aspirations and baser peccadillos, would-be-good intentions modified by a weakness for 'cakes and ale'. As he put it: "the web of life is of a mingled yarn, good and ill together." (AWEW 4.3.83) His exploration of the kaleidoscopic range of human behaviour is nowhere better displayed than in the two plays about Henry the Fourth, where we are shown, in 'the whirligig of time', a panorama of characters varying from heroes to rogues, the whole shot through with a non-judgemental humour.

A disclaimer is in order here. This book is in no way intended to be a scholarly study of Shakespeare. It is based simply upon one ordinary layman's response to the clear meaning expressed through Shakespeare's words, characters and plots. For a deeper academic analysis the reader must look elsewhere.

These introductory pages have set the scene, and provided a background for the understanding of the man and his work. Now it is time to see if he has a message for our own times and our own lives.

A note concerning the so-called ' Lost Years' :

If we accept the statement of his fellow-actor that Shakespeare had been 'a schoolmaster in the country,' an intriguing guess suggests that he spent some years in the households of two wealthy Lancashire families. There were many gentry in that county who secretly held to the old faith, and because of the danger of betrayal, they would have sought out Catholics as tutors for their children. John Cottom, a Lancashire man and a Catholic, was schoolmaster at Stratford in 1579, when his pupil William would have been 15. The theory suggests that Cottom could have recommended his bright young pupil, brought up by Catholic parents, for a post as tutor in the family of the very wealthy Catholic, Alexander Hoghton of Hoghton Hall near Preston, not far from Cottom's home, and Cottom's father was a tenant of Hoghton's. In 1581 Alexander Hoghton made a will, mentioning among others his brother, Sir Thomas Hoghton:

> ... it is my mind & will that the said Thomas Hoghton .. my brother shall have all my instruments belonging to musics, & all manner of play clothes if he bee minded to keep & do keep players. And if he will not keep & maintain players, then it is my mind & will that Sir Thomas Hesketh knight shall have the same

instruments & play clothes. And I most heartily require the said Sir Thomas to be friendly unto Fulk Gillom & William Shakeshafte now dwelling with me & either to take them unto his service or else to help them to some good master, as my trust is he will.

Why this special favour to these two men (out of 30 servants named in the will), unless they displayed unusual gifts? 'Now dwelling with me' suggests a status within the family circle. Fulk Gillom's name turns up years later as an actor in Chester. Hesketh took over his house and servants, but was arrested later that year under new anti-Catholic legislation, so presumably William 'Shakeshafte' was passed on 'to some good master', perhaps to Lancashire's Ferdinando Stanley, Lord Strange, patron of an acting company which included several players who went on to form the Chamberlain's Men, the company to which Shakespeare later belonged. It is a reasonable supposition that Shakespeare was previously one of Lord Strange's players, during which time he developed his talents as player and playwright to the foremost rank, explaining why Robert Greene attacked him so enviously in 1592 as the 'upstart crow' ... 'in his own conceit the only Shake-scene in a country'. The title page of Titus Andronicus states that it was first played by the 'servants' of Lord Derby, the title Lord Strange inherited in 1593, and it is held that there are several allusions to Lord Strange in Love's Labour's Lost.

One has to admit, however that there are several difficulties with this Lancashire theory. Surely the lawyer who drew up Hoghton's will would have been careful to write the legatee's name correctly. Also, 17-year-old William, supposedly serving only briefly in the household, was hardly mature enough to have been singled out as a major legatee, more likely to have been an older man with years of service, and there were plenty of Shakeshaftes living locally, with at least three named William.

A more credible suggestion to account for William's 'Lost Years' is that he might have served as a clerk or general dogsbody in a Stratford attorney's office. This idea stems from the frequency with which legal terms are scattered throughout the plays. There were several lawyers in Stratford who might have employed him, such as Thomas Trussell, a relative of his mother, or Henry Rogers, Town Clerk and Steward from 1570 to 1586.

An example of Shakespeare's familiarity with legal jargon is shown by Hamlet in the graveyard:

> (Ham) There's another: why may not that be the skull of a lawyer? Where be his quiddities now, his quillets, his cases, his

tenures, and his tricks? why does he suffer this rude knave now to knock him about the sconce with a dirty shovel, and will not tell him of his action of battery? Hum! This fellow might be in's time a great buyer of land, with his statutes, his recognizances, his fines, his double vouchers, his recoveries: is this the fine of his fines, and the recovery of his recoveries, to have his fine pate full of fine dirt? will his vouchers vouch him no more of his purchases, and double ones too, than the length and breath of a pair of indentures? The very conveyances of his lands will hardly lie in this box.

(Hamlet 5.1.104)

YOUTH & NATURE

The experiences of life run from the cradle to the grave, so it would seem natural to follow that same order in this book. That journey has been wonderfully and succinctly expressed by Jaques in As You Like it:

All the world's a stage,
And all the men and women merely players:
They have their exits and their entrances;
And one man in his time plays many parts,
His acts being seven ages. As, first the infant
Mewling and puking in the nurse's arms.
And then the whining schoolboy, with his satchel
And shining morning face, creeping like snail
Unwillingly to school. And then the lover,
Sighing like furnace, with a woeful ballad   (sound of bellows)
Made to his mistress' eyebrow. Then a soldier
Full of strange oaths, and bearded like the pard,   (leopard)
Jealous in honour, sudden and quick in quarrel,
Seeking the bubble reputation
Even in the cannon's mouth. And then the justice,
In fair round belly with good capon lined,
With eyes severe and beard of formal cut,
Full of wise saws and modern instances;   (saws=maxims)
And so he plays his part. The sixth age shifts
Into the lean and slipper'd pantaloon,   (Pantalone: comic figure
With spectacles on nose and pouch on side;   in Italian comedy)
His youthful hose, well saved, a world too wide
For his shrunk shank, and his big manly voice,
Turning again toward childish treble, pipes
And whistles in his sound. Last scene of all,
That ends this strange eventful history,
Is second childishness and mere oblivion,
Sans teeth, sans eyes, sans taste, sans everything.   (2.7.139)

The baptismal register for the parish of Stratford records, opposite the date 26 April 1564: "Gulielmus filius Johannes Shakspere". A baptism took place customarily three days after a birth. William was the third child and first son of John Shakespeare and his wife Mary. Five more children were yet to come.

A wry look at birth comes from King Lear:

> We came crying hither:
> Thou know'st the first time that we smell the air
> We waul and cry ...
> When we are born, we cry that we are come
> To this great stage of fools.   (4.6.183)

Relying on a few clues in the plays, we may guess that young William enjoyed a happy childhood:

> (Hermione)   Come, I'll question you
> Of my lord's tricks and yours when you were boys;
> You were pretty lordlings then?
>
> (Polixenes)   We were, fair queen,
> Two lads that thought there was no more behind
> But such a day to-morrow as today,
> And to be boy eternal.
>
> (Hermione) Was not my lord the verier wag o' the two?
> (Polixenes) We were as twinn'd lambs that did frisk i' the sun,
> And bleat the one at the other; what we changed
> Was innocence for innocence; we knew not
> The doctrine of ill-doing, no, nor dream'd
> That any did.   (WT 1.2.60)

Shakespeare has little to say about the years of adolescence, apart from making the obvious comment that 'youth is wild, and age is tame.' But his observation of the fickleness of those growing years is still true for our own day, when the young follow mindlessly after the latest craze in clothing or popular music:

> ...   there are fond   (=foolish)
> lascivious metres, to whose venom sound
> The open ear of youth doth always listen:
> Report of fashions in proud Italy (read USA?)
> Whose manners still our tardy apish nation
> Limps after in base imitation ...
> So it be new, there's no respect how vile.   (Rd II 2.1.18)

16

(these are all -)
Younger spirits, whose apprehensive senses
All but new things disdain; whose judgements are
Mere fathers of their garments; whose constancies
Expire before their fashions.   (AWEW 1.2.60)

seest thou not, I say,
What a deformed thief this fashion is?
How giddily he turns about all the hotbloods
Between fourteen and five and thirty?   (MAAN 3.3.130)

Shakespeare was born in a small country town surrounded by fields and woods in the very heart of the rural landscape of England, and he absorbed the atmosphere of it in his bones, as is abundantly clear from his numerous references to the natural scenes of the countryside. His keen eye noticed everything:

The strawberry grows underneath the nettle
And wholesome berries thrive and ripen best
Neighbour'd by fruit of baser quality   (Hy V 1.1.60)

… … … … … … … … … …
          This guest of summer,
The temple-haunting martlet, does approve, (martin? more likely, swift)
By his loved mansionry, that the heavens' breath
Smells wooingly here; no jutty, frieze,
Buttress, nor coign of vantage, but this bird
Hath made his pendent bed and procreant cradle:
Where they most breed and haunt, I have observed
The air is delicate.   (Mac 1.6.3)

Note that "I have observed." Anything once seen appears to have been retained in his extraordinary memory, to be brought out again as the occasion demanded it.

This book aims to show that Shakespeare's work can speak to our own needs and predicament, and someone may object that they cannot see that an observation of nature has any relevance to a full and balanced life. I would answer that with an emphatic yes. As we direct our gaze away from a concentration on our own petty troubles, and look outwards at the beauty of the natural world, we tend to find consolation and contentment there. Botanists and gardeners are generally more rounded and fulfilled people than your average nine-to-five commuting workaholic.

Young William took pleasure in the variety of flowers he saw around him in gardens and hedgerows:

> I know a bank whereon the wild thyme blows,
> Where oxlips and the nodding violet grows:
> Quite over-canopied with luscious woodbine,   (MND 2.1.249)
> With sweet musk roses, and with eglantine   (= sweet-brier, the wild
> rose with fragrant foliage)

Flowers are brought into his plays not as sentimental pretty ornaments, but are worked into solemn events. Here is Ophelia in her madness, after Hamlet has rejected her and killed her father:

> There's rosemary, that's for remembrance. Pray you, love, remember. And there is pansies, that's for thoughts*. There's fennel for you, and columbines. There's rue for you, and here's some for me. . . There's a daisy. I would give you some violets, but they withered all when my father died.   (4.7.174)

And later Queen Gertrude describes where poor Ophelia was found drowned:

> There is a willow grows aslant the brook   (thus F; askant in Q2)
> That shows his hoar leaves in the glassy stream: (or, hoary)
> Therewith fantastic garlands did she make,   (come, in F)
> Of crow-flowers, nettles, daises, and long purples   (loosestrife?)
> That liberal shepherds give a grosser name,
> But our cold maids do dead men's fingers call them.
> There on the pendent boughs her coronet weeds
> Clambering to hang, an envious sliver broke,
> When down her weedy trophies and herself
> Fell in the weeping brook.   (see the note at the end
> of the chapter)(4.7.166)

After Agincourt, the Duke of Burgundy deplores the effect war has had on France:

> My duty to you both, on equal love,
> Great kings of France and England!
>   … Let it not disgrace me
> If I demand before this royal view,
> What rub, or what impediment there is   (rub=obstacle)

---

*   pensées?

18

Why that the naked, poor and mangled Peace,
Dear nurse of arts, plenties, and joyful births,
Should not, in this best garden of the world,
Our fertile France, put up her lovely visage.
Alas, she hath from France too long been chased!
And all her husbandry doth lie on heaps,
Corrupting in its own fertility.
Her vine, the merry cheerer of the heart,
Unprunèd dies; her hedges even-pleached   (=neatly 'laid')
Like prisoners wildly overgrown with hair,
Put forth disordered twigs; her fallow leas
The darnel, hemlock, and rank fumitory
Doth root upon, while that the coulter rusts
That should deracinate such savagery;
The even mead, that erst brought sweetly forth
The freckled cowslip, burnet, and green clover,
Wanting the scythe, all uncorrected, rank,
Conceives by idleness, and nothing teems
But hateful docks, rough thistles, kecksies, burrs   (k= umbellifers
Losing both beauty and utility.   such as cow parsley)
And all our vineyards, fallows, meads, and hedges,
Defective in their natures, grow to wildness   (Hy V 5.2.23)

Shakespeare invents many new words to serve his purpose: in this passage 'deracinate' is used for the first time recorded. He must have read 'deraciner' in a French book.

He constantly draws metaphors from daily life to point a moral. Here in Richard II he compares a gardener's tasks with the political scene:

(Gardener:) Go, bind thou up yond dangling apricots   (apricocks-F)
Which, like unruly children, make their sire
Stoop with oppression of their prodigal weight.
Give some supportance to the bending twigs.
Go thou, and like an executioner
Cut off the heads of too-fast-growing sprays
That look too lofty in our commonwealth:
All must be even in our government.
You thus employed, I will go root away
The noisome weeds which without profit suck
The soil's fertility from wholesome flowers.
(Servant:) Why should we, in the compass of a pale   (=fence)

Keep law and form and due proportion,
Showing as in a model our firm estate,
When our sea-walled garden, the whole land,
Is full of weeds, her fairest flowers choked up,
Her fruit trees all unpruned, her hedges ruined,
Her knots disordered and her wholesome herbs   (knots=formal
Swarming with caterpillars?   flowerbeds)
(Gardener:) Hold thy peace!
He that has suffered this disordered spring
Hath now himself met with the fall of leaf.
The weeds which his broad-spreading leaves did shelter ...
    ... Are plucked up, root and all, by Bolingbroke
    ...   and Bolingbroke
Hath seized the wasteful King. O, what pity is it
That he had not so trimmed and dressed this land
As we this garden! We at time of year
Do wound the bark, the skin of our fruit trees,
Lest being over-proud in sap and blood
With too much riches it confound itself.
Had he done so to great and growing men,
They might have lived to bear, and he to taste
Their fruits of duty. Superfluous branches
We lop away that bearing boughs may live.
Had he done so, himself had borne the crown
Which waste of idle hours hath quite thrown down.   (3.4.29)

Weeds get another mention in King Lear, where Cordelia sees her father:

As mad as the vex'd sea; singing aloud
Crowned with rank fumitory and furrow-weeds,
With burdocks, hemlock, nettles, cuckoo-flowers,
Darnel, and all the idle weeds that grow
In our sustaining corn.   (4.4.2)

These somewhat sombre lines need to be balanced by something more cheerful, and no scene is more cheerful and expressive of the countryside than the sheep-shearing in the Winter's Tale. This picture of country life must be based on many similar merry gatherings which the young Shakespeare would have attended.

(Florizel, to Perdita:) See, your guests approach.

Address yourself to entertain them sprightly,
And let's be red with mirth.
(Shepherd:) Fie, daughter! When my old wife lived, upon
This day she was both pantler, butler, cook;
Both dame and servant; welcomed all, served all;
Would sing her song and dance her turn; now here,
At upper end o'th'table, now i'th'middle;
On his shoulder, and his; her face o'fire
With labour, and the thing she took to quench it:
She would to each one sip. You are retired,
As if you were a feasted one and not
The hostess of the meeting. Pray you, bid
These unknown friends to's welcome, for it is
A way to make us better friends, more known.
Come, quench your blushes and present yourself
That which you are, Mistress o'th'Feast. Come on,
And bid us welcome to your sheep-shearing,
As your good flock shall prosper.
(Perdita, to Polixenes:)   Sir, welcome.
It is my father's will I should take on me
The hostess-ship o'th'day. (to Camillo:) You're welcome, sir.
Give me those flowers there, Dorcas. Reverend sirs,
For you there's rosemary and rue; these keep
Seeming and savour all the winter long;
Grace and remembrance be to you both,
And welcome to our shearing! …
        …   The fairest flowers o 'th'season
Are our carnations and streaked gillyflowers   (=clove-scented pink)
    … …   Here's flowers for you:
Hot lavender, mints, savory, marjoram;
The marigold that goes to bed wi'the sun
And with him rises weeping; these are flowers
Of middle summer, and I think they are given
To men of middle age …
(to Florizel:) Now, my fair'st friend. (her lover)
I would have some flowers o'th'spring … Daffodils,
That come before the swallow dares, and take
The winds of March with beauty; violets, dim,
But sweeter than the lids of Juno's eyes
Or Cytherea's breath; pale primroses,   (Cytherea=Venus)

21

That die unmarried ere they can behold
Bright Phoebus in his strength ...   (Phoebus=Apollo, the sun god)
    ...   bold oxlips and
The crown imperial; lilies of all kinds,   (The crown imperial,
                                                recently introduced 1597)
The flower-de-luce being one: O, these I lack   (iris)
To make you garlands of.   (4.3.52)

After he bought New Place, the largest house in Stratford, in 1597, Shakespeare referred to gardening and garden flowers more frequently, and I like the line in Hamlet:

Do not spread the compost on the weeds
To make them ranker.   (Ham 3.4.150)

There speaks a man with a 'hands -on' knowledge of gardening.

His country upbringing, then, provided him with a thousand metaphors to be woven into his work, and that goes for his observation of the weather and the changing seasons, among which, as we might expect, Spring takes pre-eminence. We must bear in mind, however, that in Shakespeare's time, owing to an unreformed error in the Julian Calendar, the Spring Equinox fell on a date some ten days earlier than with us today, so his late April would have a similar temperature to that of early May in the 21st century. Here, then, are lines which celebrate Spring:

Welcome hither
As is the Spring to the earth   (WT 5.1.150)
... ...
As full of spirit as the month of May   (1 Hy IV 4.1.101)
    ... ...
The uncertain glory of an April day   (TGV 1.3.85)
    ... ...
From you have I been absent in the Spring,   (Son 98)
When proud-pied April, dressed in all his trim   (=multi-coloured)
Hath put a spirit of youth in everything
        ... ...
Well-apparelled April on the heel
Of limping winter treads   (R&J 1.2.27)

That is a good example of the compressed metaphors to be found throughout the plays. Of course, the month of April is not in reality dressed in clothing, nor is it capable of treading on any part of winter, which has no heel, and cannot limp. But what a powerful picture is con-

veyed to the imagination! Amid the rich abundance of seasonal metaphors there is only space to quote a few:

> Your tongue's sweet air
> More tuneable than lark to shepherd's ear,
> When wheat is green, when hawthorn buds appear. (MND 1.1.182)
>
> ... ...
>
> To me, fair friend, you never can be old,
> For as you were when first your eye I eyed,
> Such seems your beauty still. Three winters cold
> Have from the forests shook three summers' pride,
> Three beauteous springs to yellow autumn turned
> In process of the seasons have I seen,
> Three April perfumes in three hot Junes burned,
> Since first I saw you fresh, which yet are green ...   (Son 104)
>
> ... ...

And under the seasonal heading comes the most memorable line of
them all:

> Shall I compare thee to a summer's day?
> Thou art more lovely and more temperate:
> Rough winds do shake the darling buds of May,
> And summer's lease hath all too short a date:
> Sometime too hot the eye of heaven shines,
> And often is his gold complexion dimmed;
> And every fair from fair sometime declines,
> By chance, or nature's changing course untrimmed;
> But thy eternal summer shall not fade ...   (Son 18)

> Some people show winter in their glum looks:
> What's the matter
> That you have such a February face,
> So full of frost, of storm, and cloudiness?   (MAAN 5.4.20)

In the song Spring and Winter from Love's Labour's Lost he conveys
country scenes so vividly that you fancy you saw them yourself:

Spring

> When daisies pied and violets blue,
> And lady-smocks all silver-white,
> And cuckoo-buds of yellow hue
> Do paint the meadows with delight,

23

The cuckoo then, on every tree,
Mocks married men; for thus sings he,
                    Cuckoo!
Cuckoo, cuckoo! – O word of fear,
Unpleasing to a married ear!
When shepherds pipe on oaten straws,
And merry larks are ploughman's clocks,
When turtles tread, and rooks, and daws,   (turtle doves)
And maidens bleach their summer smocks
The cuckoo then, on every tree,
Mocks married men; for thus sings he,
                    Cuckoo!
Cuckoo, cuckoo! – O word of fear,
Unpleasing to a married ear!

Winter
When icicles hang by the wall,
And Dick the shepherd blows his nail,
And Tom bears logs into the hall,
And milk comes frozen home in pail,
When blood is nipp'd, and ways be foul,
Then nightly sings the staring owl,
                    To-whit!
To-who! – a merry note,
While greasy Joan doth keel the pot.
When all aloud the wind doth blow,
And coughing drowns the parson's saw,
And birds sit brooding in the snow,
And Marians' nose looks red and raw,
When roasted crabs hiss in the bowl,   (crabapples)
Then nightly sings the staring owl,
                    To-whit!
To-who! – a merry note,
While greasy Joan doth keel the pot.   (keel=skim)   (5.2.902)

As a country boy, he noticed with a keen eye the colours and atmosphere of the changing moods of day and night. One should remember
that Shakespeare's stage had no scenery, so the actor had to set the scene
in words, indicating to the audience the time of day.

Dawn seems to have been a favourite time of day for him:

> Good morrow, masters, put your torches out;
> The wolves have preyed, and look, the gentle day,
> Before the wheels of Phoebus, round about   (=chariot of sun-god)
> Dapples the drowsy east with spots of grey.   (MAAN 5.3.24)

> The grey-eyed morn smiles on the frowning night
> Chequering the eastern clouds with streaks of light;
> And flecked darkness, like a drunkard, reels
> From forth day's path and Titan's fiery wheels.   (R&J 2.2.188)

> Full many a glorious morning I have seen
> Flatter the mountain-tops with sovereign eye
> Kissing with golden face the meadows green
> Gilding pale streams with heavenly alchemy.   (Son 33)

> envious streaks
> Do lace the severing clouds in yonder east:
> Night's candles are burnt out, and jocund day
> Stands tiptoe on the misty mountain tops.   (R&J 3.5.7)

As we repeat those last lines, we know they were the creation of a supreme poet.

> Lo! here the gentle lark, weary of rest,
> From his moist cabinet mounts up on high,
> And wakes the morning, from whose silver breast
> The sun ariseth in his majesty,
> Who doth the world so gloriously behold,
> The cedar-tops and hills seem burnished gold.   (V&A 853)

There are twenty seven references to larks in his works – he must have been an early riser!

In Henry V, the French nobility, impatient at the slow pace of time during the night before the battle, complain "Will it never be day?" – but then, when the dawn breaks, we get the splendid line:

> The sun doth gild our armour. Up, my lords!   (4.2.1)

With the same verbal felicity with which Shakespeare conveys the atmosphere of dawn, so he is able to picture the onset of night and the hours of darkness.

In a Midsummer Night's Dream night time has a magical quality under the light of the moon, though it would seem a new moon, described here with an apt simile:

> the moon, like to a silver bow
> New-bent in heaven (1.1.9)

Since this play is a fantastic dream, we must not be surprised when the moon waxes rapidly and is able to light the earth:

> when Phoebe doth behold (=the moon)
> Her silver visage in the watery glass
> Decking with liquid pearl the bladed grass. (1.1.209)

But the most memorable of Shakespeare's night-time scenes is the Merchant of Venice, when Lorenzo and Jessica declare their love beneath a canopy of stars:

> (Lorenzo:) The moon shines bright: in such a night as this,
> When the sweet wind did gently kiss the trees
> And they did make no noise, in such a night
> Troilus methinks mounted the Troyan walls,
> And sighed his soul toward the Grecian tents,
> Where Cressid lay that night.
> (Jessica:)   In such a night
> Did Thisbe fearfully o'ertrip the dew,
> And saw the lion's shadow ere himself,
> And ran dismayed away.
> (Lorenzo:)   In such a night
> Stood Dido with a willow in her hand   (=symbol of forsaken love)
> Upon the wild sea-banks, and waft her love
> To come again to Carthage.
> (Jessica:)   In such a night
> Medea gathered the enchanted herbs
> That did renew old Aeson.   (=father of Jason)
> (Lorenzo:)   In such a night
> Did Jessica steal from the wealthy Jew,
> And with an unthrift love did run from Venice,
> As far as Belmont.
> (Jessica:)   In such a night
> Did young Lorenzo swear he loved her well,
> Stealing her soul with many vows of faith,
> And ne'er a true one.

(Lorenzo:)   In such a night
Did pretty Jessica, like a little shrew,
Slander her love, and he forgave her.
                    (enter Stephano)

… … … … … …

(Lorenzo:) My friend Stephano, signify, I pray you,
Within the house, your mistress is at hand,
And bring the music forth into the air.

… … … … … … … …

How sweet the moonlight sleeps upon this bank!
Here will we sit, and let the sounds of music
Creep in our ears; soft stillness and the night
Become the touches of sweet harmony.   (=suit, befit)
Sit, Jessica: look how the floor of heaven
Is thick inlaid with patines of bright gold:
There's not the smallest orb which thou behold'st
But in his motion like an angel sings,
Still quiring to the young-eyed cherubins;
Such harmony is in immortal souls;
But, whilst this muddy vesture of decay
Doth grossly close it in, we cannot hear it
                    (Enter Musicians)

… … … … … … … …

The man that hath no music in himself,
Nor is not moved with concord of sweet sounds,
Is fit for treasons, stratagems and spoils;
The motions of his spirit are as dull as night,
And his affections dark as Erebus: (= dark cave, entrance to hell)
Let no such man be trusted.   (5.1.1)

Night-time has more sinister associations in the tragedies:
    Light thickens, and the crow
    Makes wing to the rooky wood
    The west yet glimmers with some streaks of day:
    Now spurs the lated traveller apace   (belated)
    To gain the timely inn.   (Mac 3.2.50)

    … … … … … … … …

    'Tis now the very witching time of night,
    When churchyards yawn, and hell itself breathes out
    Contagion to this world: now could I drink hot blood,

And do such bitter business as the day
Would quake to look on. (Ham 3.1.413)

… … … … … … … …

know'st thou not
That when the searching eye of heaven is hid
Behind the globe that lights the lower world,
Then thieves and robbers range abroad unseen,
In murders and in outrage, boldly here;
But when, from under this terrestrial ball,
He fires the proud tops of the eastern pines,
And darts his light through every guilty hole,
Then murders, treasons, and detested sins,
The cloak of night being plucked from off their backs,
Stand bare and naked, trembling at themselves. (Rd II 3.2.36)

These word-pictures of times and seasons may be the creation of Shakespeare's maturity, but the keen observation upon which they are based must go back to that watchful boy wandering through the fields, taking delight in the changing face of nature.

The pastoral idyll of his youth is recreated in one of his most enjoyable and enchanting plays, As You Like It. Shakespeare took someone else's story, a romance called Rosalynde by Thomas Lodge (1590), and transformed it into the play we know. Even the title was stolen, for in the preface to Rosalynde the author wrote: "If you like it, so". Shakespeare follows Lodge in setting the play in the Forest of the Ardennes, but in calling it Arden he must have been thinking with affection of his own local Forest of Arden. In the play, Duke Senior is banished by his usurping brother, and takes refuge in the Forest of Arden, and Shakespeare gives the strong impression that the life in the forest is preferable to the life in the court.

- Where will the old Duke live?
- They say he is already in the Forest of Arden, and a many merry men with him; and there they live like the old Robin Hood of England. They say many young gentlemen flock to him every day, and fleet the time carelessly as they did in the golden world. (AYLI 1.1.121)

The Golden Age was a mythical age of innocence, analogous to the Garden of Eden.

The remains of the ancient Forest of Arden lay to the north of Stratford. The memory of it is preserved even today in place-names such as Henley-in-Arden and Tanworth-in Arden. The topographer William Camden, writing during the 1580s, noted the contrast between the Feldon, 'fielden' farmland south of Stratford, and Arden to the north of the town: "The Feldon lieth on this side Avon, southward, a plain champaign country, . . rich in corn and green grass … a right goodly and pleasant prospect." He goes on "Now let us enter the woodland, which beyond the River Avon spreadeth itself northward much larger in compass than the Feldon, and is for the most part thick set with woods, and yet not without pastures, cornfields and sundry mines of iron."

Arden meant more than the forest to William, for his mother was Mary Arden, descended from a family prominent in that area since Saxon times.

In setting the location of As You Like It in his own Forest of Arden he is consciously and deliberately returning to the scenes of his youth. Perhaps he was glad to escape, even in imagination, away from the turmoil and corruption of London.

> (Duke Senior, in the forest:)
> Now, my co-mates and brothers in exile,
> Hath not old custom made this life more sweet
> Than that of painted pomp? Are not these woods
> More free from peril than the envious court?
> Here feel we but the penalty of Adam,   (but: not in F)
> The season's difference; as, the icy fang
> And churlish chiding of the winter's wind,
> Which, when it bites and blows upon my body,
> Even till I shrink with cold, I smile and say
> 'This is no flattery: these are counsellors
> That feelingly persuade me what I am.'
> Sweet are the uses of adversity, …
> … And this our life exempt from public haunt,
> Finds tongues in trees, books in the running brooks,
> Sermons in stones, and good in every thing:
> I would not change it.   (this line spoken by Amiens in Folio)
>   (AYLI 2.1.1)

Later, Amiens, one of the Duke's companions, celebrates their new way of life in songs:

> Under the greenwood tree
> Who loves to lie with me,

And turn his merry note
Unto the sweet bird's throat,
Come hither, come hither, come hither:
      Here shall he see
      No enemy
But winter and rough weather.

Who doth ambition shun,
And loves to live i'the sun,
Seeking the food he eats,
And pleased with what he gets,
Come hither, come hither, come hither:
      Here shall he see
      No enemy
But winter and rough weather.   (2.5.1)
. ...
Blow, blow, thou winter wind,
Thou art not so unkind
As man's ingratitude:
Thy tooth is not so keen,
Because thou art not seen,
Although thy breath be rude.
Heigh-ho! sing, heigh-ho! unto the green holly:
Most friendship is feigning, most loving mere folly.
Then heigh-ho! the holly!
This life is most jolly.   (2.7.174)

This concept of the simple life, the ideal life, derived from the Arcadia of Shakespeare's rural childhood, may be seen in the Tempest, his last play. There he created a mythical island, with Prospero, a magician (the author?) who is able to control everything that happens there. As with the Forest of Arden, is the world-weary dramatist returning in imagination to the idyllic scenes of his formative years? He may have derived the idea of such an island from reading Thomas More's Utopia, published in English in 1551, and the concept of a desert island upon which an author may build a blueprint for a commonwealth recurs in many forms in the history of literature, from Robinson Crusoe via Lilliput and Erewhon to Brave New World – a title taken from the Tempest. The immediate inspiration for the Tempest was an account of the Sea venture, a ship heading for Virginia in 1609, only to be overwhelmed by a great storm, and wrecked on the shores of Bermuda – the "still-vexed Bermoothes" of the play. As in the play, all on board survived.

The good old loyal courtier of the play is Gonzalo, and Shakespeare puts into his mouth an exposition of an ideal state, but, perhaps deliberately, he makes sure it is scoffed at by the amoral cynics around him:

> (Gonzalo:) Had I a plantation of this isle, my lord –
> (Antonio:) He'd sow it with nettle-seed.
> (Sebastian:)   Or docks, or mallows.
> (Gon:) – And were the king on't, what would I do?
> (Seb:) -'Scape being drunk, for want of wine.
> (Gon:) I' the commonwealth, I would by contraries
> Execute all things: for no kind of traffic   (=trade)
> Would I admit; no name of magistrate;
> Letters should not be known; riches, poverty,
> And use of service, none; contract, succession,
> Bourn, bound of land, tilth, vineyard, none;
> No use of metal, corn, or wine, or oil;
> No occupation; all men idle, all;
> And women too; but innocent and pure;
> No sovereignty;-
> (Seb:)   And yet he would be king on't.
> (Ant:) The latter end of his commonwealth forgets the beginning.
> (Gon:) All things in common nature should produce
> Without sweat or endeavour: treason, felony,
> Sword, pike, knife, gun, or need of any engine,   (engine=cannon
> Would I not have; but nature should bring forth,   on wheels)
> Of its own kind, all foison, all abundance,   (=plenty)
> To feed my innocent people.
> (Seb:) No marrying 'mong his subjects?
> (Ant:) None man; all idle; whores and knaves.
> (Gon:) I would with such perfection govern, sir,
> To excel the golden age.
> (Seb:)   Save his majesty!
> (Ant:) Long Live Gonzalo!   (see the note at the end of the chapter)
>   (2.1.148)

William Strachey's account of the shipwreck on Bermuda seems to have provided Shakespeare with other material for his play: the phenomenon of St. Elmo's fire in the ship's rigging, the means of subsistence to be found on the island, and a suppressed mutiny.

Strachey's account mentions a previous description of Bermuda by one Oviedo, whose first names were Gonzalo Ferdinando – names found in the play. Was this coincidence, or Shakespeare's retentive memory? The 'man-monster' Caliban may personify the simplicity of the native Indians of the New World. The name suggests Carib and cannibal. Caliban complains that

> This island's mine …
> Which thou tak'st from me. When thou camest first,
> Thou strok'dst me, and mad'st much of me; would'st give me
> Water with berries in't; and teach me how
> To name the bigger light, and how the less,
> That burn by day and night: and then I lov'd thee
> And showed thee all the qualities o'th'isle,
> The fresh springs, brine-pits, barren place, and fertile.
> Cursed be I that did so! …
> For I am all the subjects that you have,
> Which first was mine own king.   (1.2.331)

That passage seems to foreshadow the age of English colonialism, then in its infancy.

Caliban, the child of nature, is the expert at survival in the natural environment, and seeks to pass that knowledge on to the shipwrecked mariners:

> I'll show thee every fertile inch o' the island …
> … I'll show thee the best springs; I'll pluck thee berries;
> I'll fish for thee, and get thee wood enough …
> … I prithee, let me bring you where crabs grow;   (crabs=crabapples)
> And I with my long nails will dig thee pig-nuts;
> Show thee a jay's nest and instruct thee how
> To snare the nimble marmoset; I'll bring thee
> To clust'ring filberts, and sometimes I'll get thee
> Young seamells from the rock. Wilt thou go with me?   (=seagulls)
>   (2.2.160)

One of the most beautiful passages in the play is put into the mouth of Caliban, the savage with his ear close to nature:

> Be not afeard: the isle is full of noises,
> Sounds and sweet airs, that give delight, and hurt not.
> Sometimes a thousand twangling instruments
> Will hum about mine ears; and sometimes voices,

That, if I then had wak'd after long sleep,
Will make me sleep again: and then, in dreaming,
The clouds methought would open and show riches
Ready to drop upon me; that, when I wak'd
I cried to dream again.   (3.2.147)

In quoting all these excerpts, I am asserting that this celebration of
the simplicity and beauty of nature comes directly from young William's
appreciation of his rural surroundings, and to clinch my argument I end
with Ariel's song from the Tempest:

Where the bee sucks, there suck I
In a cowslip's bell I lie;
There I couch when owls do cry.
On the bat's back I do fly
After summer merrily;
Merrily, merrily shall I live now
Under the blossom that hangs on the bough.   (5.1.88)

And we must not omit that famous song of Ariel's, full of magic and
mystery:

Full fathom five thy father lies;
Of his bones are coral made;
Those are pearls that were his eyes;
Nothing of him that doth fade,
But doth suffer a sea-change,
Into something rich and strange.
Sea -nymphs hourly ring his knell:
Hark! now I hear them – ding – dong – bell.   (1.2.399)

The deeper significance of what happens in the Tempest is considered later in this book.

During his childhood Shakespeare observed closely the variety of
animals and birds around him, for images based on them are woven in
to all his work.

When they him spy,
As wild geese that the creeping fowler eye,
Or russet-pated choughs, many in sort,
Rising and cawing at the gun's report,
Sever themselves, and madly sweep the sky,
So at his sight away his fellows fly.   (MND 3.2.19)

33

... ...
I see you stand like greyhounds in the slips
Straining upon the start. The game's afoot!   (Hy V 3.1.31)

... ...
                    The poor wren,
The most diminutive of birds, will fight,
Her young ones in her nest, against the owl.   (Mac 4.2.9)

Shakespeare had a close relationship with domestic animals, for his father was a glove-maker, and dealt in wool, and perhaps in skins and meat. No doubt young William began his working life assisting his father, and he brings knowledge of glove-making into the plays. There are frequent references to butchers and slaughter houses throughout his work, and repetition of the word 'blood' is a sinister theme, especially in Macbeth. Aubrey related a story about young Shakespeare that " his father was a butcher, and I have been told heretofore by some of the neighbours, that when he was a boy he exercised his father's trade, but when he killed a calf he would do it in a high style and make a speech." That story, however, cannot be reconciled with the many passages in his work which demonstrate his compassion for animals, as the following excerpts prove:

        And as the butcher takes away the calf,
        And binds the wretch, and beats it when it strays,
        Bearing it to the bloody slaughter-house;
        Even so, remorseless, have they borne him hence:
        And as the dam runs lowing up and down,
        Looking the way her harmless young one went,
        And can do naught but wail her darling's loss;
        Even so myself bewails good Gloucester's case
        With sad unhelpful tears; and with dimmed eyes
        Look after him, and cannot do him good,
        So mighty are his vowèd enemies.   (2 Hy VI 3.1.210)

In Venus and Adonis his sympathies lie all with the hunted, not the hunters. Here he pities "the timorous flying hare:"

        Mark the poor wretch, to overshoot his troubles,
        How he outruns the wind, and with what care
        He cranks and crosses, with a thousand doubles;
        The many musits through which he goes   (=gap in hedge)
        Are like a labyrinth to amaze his foes ...

34

... By this, poor Wat, far off upon a hill,
Stands on his hinder legs with listening ear,
To hearken if his foes pursue him still;
Anon their loud alarums he doth hear,
And now his grief may be comparèd well
To one sore sick that hears the passing bell.
Then shalt thou see the dew-bedabbled wretch
Turn and return, indenting with the way;
Each envious briar his weary legs doth scratch,
Each shadow makes him stop, each murmur stay:
For misery is trodden on by many,
And being low never relieved by any.   (680)

He is moved to sympathy wherever he sees pain
    The bird that hath been limèd in a bush
    With trembling wings misdoubteth every bush.   (2 Hy VI 5.6.13)

    ... ...
    the poor beetle that we tread upon,
    In corporal sufferance finds a pang as great
    As when a giant dies.   (MFM 3.1.76)

    ... ...
    . . as the snail, whose tender horns being hit,
    Shrinks backward in his shelly cave with pain,
    And there, all smothered up, in shade doth sit,
    Long after fearing to creep forth again.   (V&A 1033)

Jaques , the gloomy philosopher in the Forest of Arden, has doubts
about the morality of the deer-hunt:
    (Duke Senior:) Come, shall we go and kill us venison?
    And yet it irks me, the poor dappled fools,
    Being native burghers of this desert city,
    Should, in their own confines, with forkèd heads,
    Have their round haunches gored.
    (Lord:)   Indeed, my lord,
    The melancholy Jaques grieves at that;
    And, in that kind, swears you do more usurp
    Than doth your brother, that hath banished you.
    Today my lord of Amiens and myself
    Did steal behind him as he lay along
    Under an oak, whose antique root peeps out

Upon the brook that brawls along this wood:
To the which place a poor sequestered stag,
That from the hunters' aim had ta'en a hurt,
Did come to languish; and indeed my lord
The wretched animal heaved forth such groans,
That their discharge did stretch his leathern coat
Almost to bursting; and the big round tears
Coursed one another down his innocent nose
In piteous chase: and thus the hairy fool,
Much marked of the melancholy Jaques,
Stood on the extremest verge of the swift brook,
Augmenting it with tears.   ...
    ...   anon, a careless herd,
Full of the pasture, jumps by with him,
And never stays to greet him; Ay, quoth Jaques,
Sweep on, you fat and greasy citizens;
'Tis just the fashion: wherefore do you look
Upon that poor and broken bankrupt there?
Thus most invectively he pierceth through
The body of the country, city, court,
Yea, and most of this our life: swearing that we
Are mere usurpers, tyrants, and what's worse
To fright the animals, and to kill them up
In their assigned and native dwelling place.   (AYLI 2.1.21)

Notes Page 14 : note on the death of Ophelia: in the passage beginning 'There is a willow grows aslant the brook. .' Shakespeare must have known about a drowning that took place in the River Avon near Stratford in 1579. One Katherine Hamlett - note the name – went with a bucket to the river to take water from it, but slipped in and was drowned. On the many occasions when I have rowed on the River Avon I have thought of this passage when avoiding the leaves of a particularly large willow which leans far over the stream, some quarter mile upstream from Stratford's ancient stone bridge.

Page 23 : Shakespeare's nostalgia for the rural idyll of his youth finds expression through the mouth of Corin, one of the shepherds in As You Like It, echoing Amiens' song:

Sir, I am a true labourer: I earn that I eat, get that I wear; owe no man hate, envy no man's happiness; glad of other men's good, content with my harm; and the greatest of my pride is to see my ewes graze and my lambs suck. (3.2.78)

Page 24 : note on Gonzalo's commonwealth:

In this passage Shakespeare echoes Montaigne's essay 'Of the Caniballes' (John Florio's translation, 1603). The copy in the British Library bears Shakespeare's signature.

It is a nation ... that hath no kinde of traffike, no knowledge of Letter, no intelligence of numbers, no name of magistrate, nor of politike superioritie, no use of service, of riches or of povertie; no contracts, no successions, no partitions, no occupation but idle; no respect of kindred, but common, no apparel but naturall, no manuring of lands, no use of wine, corne, or mettle ...

"And then the lover"

The description we have given of the country scenes of Shakespeare's youth leads naturally to the next phase of life, and the most important: falling in love. This is a strange disease like no other. Rational thought is suspended: geese are seen as swans. Volcanic energies are set in motion. Moods swing violently from one extreme to the other. And woven through it all is the urge for sexual consummation, which sometimes becomes detached from romance and is pursued for its own sake.

The themes of most plays and novels in world literature circle around lovers and their follies, their demands and their infidelities. All these aspects of love, and more, are found throughout Shakespeare's plays. Lovers are always the central figures in the comedies, and love (or sex) is the main issue in Romeo and Juliet, Antony and Cleopatra, Troilus and Cressida, Measure for Measure, and jealousy destroys Othello, and drives the plot of The Winter's Tale. In Henry the Eighth, love changes the course of history. And, of course, love (or sex) is the sole subject of the sonnets and the long poems, Venus and Adonis and the Rape of Lucrece. At this point it may be stating the obvious to say that, because of the taboos and the laws of the Elizabethan age, we will not find in the plays any mention of homosexuality, or explicit details of exotic sexual practices.

Nevertheless, sexual ambiguity always went down well with audiences, as we see, in several of the comedies, when women dress and behave as men. But hang on – weren't these women really young men anyway? No wonder the audiences laughed.

It is more than likely that it was during the spring of 1582 that young William, at the age of eighteen, fell in love with Anne Hathaway of Shottery, who was eight years his senior. What is certain is that he got her pregnant by the end of August, for their first child, Susanna, was born towards the end of May 1583, six months after their marriage in the previous November. There is a passage in The Winter's Tale where the shepherd comments on the wildness of youth and sexual liaison outside wedlock:

I would there were no age between ten and three-and-twenty,

or that youth would sleep out the rest; for there is nothing
in the between but getting wenches with child, wronging the
ancientry, stealing, fighting ...
(at that point he discovers the abandoned baby:)
What have we here? (Taking up the child) Mercy on us, a barne;
a very pretty barne! (=bairn) A boy or a child, I wonder?
A pretty one; a very pretty one; sure, some scape: though I
am not bookish, yet I can read waiting-gentlewoman in the scape.
This has been some stair-work, some trunk-work, some behind-
door work; they were warmer that got this than the poor thing
is here. I'll take it up for pity.   (3.3.58)

When Shakespeare became a father of attractive daughters, he may
have become more cautious about pre-marital sex, for in the Tempest,
as Prospero agrees to a marriage between his daughter Miranda and her
lover Ferdinand, he warns him:
Then as my gift and thine own acquisition
Worthily purchased, take my daughter: but
If thou dost break her virgin knot before
All sanctimonious ceremonies may,
With full and holy rite be ministered,
No sweet aspersion shall the heavens let fall
To make this contract grow; but barren hate,
Sour-eyed disdain and discord shall bestrew
The union of your bed with weeds so loathly
That you shall hate it both: therefore take heed,
As Hymen's lamps shall light you.   (4.1.13)

The songs in the plays set the scenes where lovers meet:
(Shakespeare chose this song for As You Like It, but the words are not his.)
It was a lover and his lass,   (AYLI 5.3.18)
        With a hey, and a ho, and a hey nonino,
That o'er the green corn-field did pass
        In the spring time, the only pretty ring time,
When birds do sing, hey ding a ding, ding;
Sweet lovers love the spring.

Between the acres of the rye,
        With a hey, and a ho, and a hey nonino,
These pretty country folks would lie,

In the spring time, the only pretty ring time,
When birds do sing, hey ding a ding, ding;
Sweet lovers love the spring.

This carol they began that hour,
      With a hey, and a ho, and a hey nonino,
How that life was but a flower
      In the spring time, the only pretty ring time,
When birds do sing, hey ding a ding, ding;
Sweet lovers love the spring.

And, therefore, take the present
      With a hey, and a ho, and a hey nonino,
For love is crownèd with the prime
      In the spring time, the only pretty ring time,
When birds do sing, hey ding a ding, ding;
Sweet lovers love the spring.

... ...

O mistress mine, where are you roaming?
O, stay and hear! your true love's coming,
That can sing both high and low:
Trip no further, pretty sweeting;
Journeys end in lovers meeting,
Every wise man's son doth know.

What is love? 'tis not hereafter;
Present mirth hath present laughter;
What's to come is still unsure:
In delay there lies no plenty;
Then come kiss me, sweet-and-twenty!
Youth's a stuff will not endure.   (TN 2.3.42)

... ...
Away before me to sweet beds of flowers;
Love-thoughts lie rich when canopied with bowers   (TN 1.1.41)

... ...
      If ever thou shalt love,
In the sweet pangs of it remember me;
For such as I am all true lovers are,

Unstaid and skittish in all motions else
Save in the constant image of the creature
That is beloved. (TN 4.1.15)

... ...

Benedick ridicules love, and looks likely to remain single:
> I do much wonder, that one man seeing how much another man is
> a fool when he dedicates his behaviours to love, will after he hath
> laughed at such shallow follies in others, become the argument
> of his own scorn by falling in love. And such a man is Claudio.
> I have known when there was no music with him but the drum
> and the fife, and now had he rather hear the tabor and the pipe.
> I have known when he would have walked ten mile afoot to see
> a good armour, and now will he lie ten nights awake carving the
> fashion of a new doublet. He was wont to speak plain and to the
> purpose, like an honest man and a soldier, and now he is turned
> orthography – his words are a very fantastical banquet, just so
> many strange dishes. May I be so converted, and see with these
> eyes? I cannot tell; I think not: I will not be sworn but Love may
> transform me to an oyster; but I'll take my oath on it, till he have
> made an oyster of me he shall never make me such a fool. One
> woman is fair, yet I am well; another is wise, yet I am well; an-
> other virtuous, yet I am well; but till all graces be in one woman,
> one woman shall not come in my grace. Rich she shall be, that's
> certain; wise, or I'll none; virtuous, or I'll never cheapen her; fair,
> or I'll never look on her; mild, or come not near me; noble, or not
> I for an angel; of good discourse, an excellent musician, and her
> hair shall be of what colour it please God. (MAAN 2.3.7)

But, in the end Benedick, the confirmed misogynist, succumbs:
> (Claudio:) If he be not in love with some woman there is no be-
> lieving old signs: a' brushes his hat o'mornings: what should
> that bode?
> (Don Pedro:) Hath any man seen him at the barber's?
> (Claudio:) No, but the barber's man hath been seen with him, and
> the old ornament of his cheek hath already stuffed tennis-balls.
> (Leonato:) Indeed he looks younger than he did, by the loss of a
> beard.
> (Don Pedro:) Nay, a' rubs himself with civet: can you smell him
> out by that? (perfume obtained from civet cat)

41

(Claudio:) That's as much as to say the sweet youth's in love.

(Don Pedro:) The greatest note of it is his melancholy.

(Claudio:) And when was he wont to wash his face?

(Don Pedro:) Yea, or to paint himself? ...

(Claudio:) Nay, but his jesting spirit, which is now crept into a lute.string, and new-governed by stops.

(Don Pedro:) Indeed, that tells a heavy tale for him. Conclude, conclude he is in love. (MAAN 3.2.37)

And what are the symptoms of love? –

(Valentine:) Why, how know you that I am in love?

(Speed:) Marry, by these special marks: first, you have learned, like Sir Proteus, to wreathe your arms like a malcontent; to relish a love-song, like a robin-redbreast; to walk alone like one that had the pestilence; to sigh, like a schoolboy that had lost his ABC; to weep, like a young wench that had buried her grandam; to fast, like one that takes diet; to watch, like one that fears robbing; to speak puling, like a beggar at Hallowmas. You were wont, when you laughed, to crow like a cock; when you walked, to walk like one of the lions; when you fasted, it was presently after dinner; when you looked sadly, it was for want of money; and now you are metamorphosed with a mistress, that, when I look on you, I can hardly think you my master. (TGV 2.1.18)

Rosalind, disguised as a young man, teases her lover, Orlando:

(Orlando:) I am he that is so love-shaked: I pray you, tell me your remedy.

(Rosalind:) There is none of my uncle's marks upon you; he taught me how to know a man in love; in which cage of rushes I am sure you are not prisoner.

(Orlando:) What were his marks?

(Rosalind:) A lean cheek, which you have not, a blue eye and sunken, which you have not, an unquestionable* spirit, which you have not ... then your hose should be ungartered, your bonnet unbanded, your sleeve unbuttoned, your shoe untied and everything about you demonstrating a careless desolation.

(AYLI 3.2.390)

---

*   averse to being questioned

Later, she teases him further:

> Come, woo me, woo me; for now I am in a holiday humour,
> and like enough to consent. (4.1.70)

Lest the atmosphere of love should become too solemn, cloying and intense, we need to insert some extracts calculated to entertain the onlookers and to appeal to the cynics. The following come from The Merry Wives of Windsor:

First we have Falstaff, the would-be seducer:

> (Fal:) My honest lads, I will tell you what I am about.
> (Pistol:) Two yards, and more.
> (Fal:) No quips now, Pistol. Indeed I am in the waist two yards about: but I am now about no waste; I am about thrift. Briefly, I do mean to make love to Ford's wife; I spy entertainment in her; she discourses, she carves, she gives the leer of invitation: I can construe the action of her familiar style; and the hardest voice of her behaviour, to be English'd rightly, is, I am Sir John Falstaff's. ...
> Now, the report goes she has all the rule of her husband's purse ...
> ... I have writ me here a letter to her: and here another to Page's wife; who even now gave me good eyes too, examined my parts with most judicious oeilliades: (amorous looks) sometimes the beam of her view gilded my foot, sometimes my portly belly.
> (Pistol:) Then did the sun on dunghill shine ...
> (Fal:) O, she did so course o'er my exteriors with such a greedy intention, that the appetite of her eye did seem to scorch me up like a burning-glass! Here's another letter to her: she bears the purse too; she is a region in Guiana, all gold and bounty. I will be cheater (=collecting officer) to them both, and they shall be exchequers to me; they shall be my East and West Indies, and I will trade to them both. Go, bear thou this letter to Mistress Page; and thou this to Mistress Ford; we will thrive, lads, we will thrive ...
> (Nym:) I will run no base humour: here, take the humour letter; I will keep the 'haviour of reputation.
> (Fal:) (to Robin) Hold, sirrah, bear you these letters tightly; Sail like my pinnace to these golden shores. (MWW 1.3.36)

And an arranged marriage:

> (Shallow:) Will you, upon good dowry, marry her?
> (Slender:) I will do a greater thing than that, upon your request, cousin, in any reason.

(Shallow:) Nay, conceive me, conceive me, sweet coz: what I do is to pleasure you, coz. Can you love the maid?

(Slender:) I will marry her, sir, at your request; but if there be no great love in the beginning, yet heaven may decrease it upon better acquaintance, when we are married and have more occasion to know one another: I hope, upon familiarity will grow more contempt: but if you say, 'Marry her,' I will marry her; that I am freely dissolved, and dissolutely… … (MWW 1.1.219)

… … … … … … … … … …

(Mistress Quickly:) Hark ye; Master Slender would speak a word with you.

(Ann Page:) I come to him. (Aside:) This is my father's choice. O, what a world of vile ill-favoured faults looks handsome in three hundred pounds a year!…

. … Good mother, do not marry me to yond fool… I'd rather be set quick i' the earth, and bowled to death with turnips. (MWW 3.4.29)

After Agincourt King Henry V, a plain blunt soldier, woos Katherine, daughter of the King of France:

(King Henry:) Fair Katherine, and most fair! Will you vouchsafe to teach a soldier terms such as will enter at a lady's ear, and plead his love suit to her gentle heart?

(Katherine:) Your majesty shall mock at me; I cannot speak your England.

(King Henry:) O fair Katherine, if you will love me soundly with your French heart, I will be glad to hear you express it brokenly with your English tongue…

… I know no ways to mince it in love, but directly to say 'I love you.' Then if you urge me farther than to say 'Do you in faith?' I wear out my suit. Give me your answer, i' faith, do; and so clap hands, and a bargain. How say you, lady?

(Katherine:) Sauf votre honneur, me understand well.

(King Henry:) Marry, if you would put me to verses or to dance for your sake, Kate, why, you undid me … If I could win a lady at leap-frog, or by vaulting into my saddle with my armour on my back, under the correction of bragging be it spoken, I should quickly leap into a wife… But, before God, Kate, I cannot look greenly, nor gasp out my eloquence, nor I have no cunning in protestation: only downright oaths, which I never use till urged, nor never break for urging. … I speak to thee plain soldier: if thou canst love me for this, take me … .And while thou liv'st, dear Kate, take a fellow of plain and uncoined constancy, for he must perforce do thee right, because he hath not the gift to woo in other places; for these fellows of infinite tongue, that can rhyme themselves into ladies' favours, they do always reason themselves out again. What! A speaker is but a prater; a rhyme is but a ballad; a good leg will fall, a straight back will stoop, a black beard will turn white, a curled pate will grow bald, a fair face will wither, a full eye will wax hollow: but a good heart, Kate, is the sun and the moon, or rather, the sun, and not the moon, for it shines bright and never changes, but keeps his course truly. If thou would have such a one, take me; and take me, take a soldier; take a soldier, take a king. And what say'st thou then to my love?   (5.2.98)

Hamlet suffers the extreme pangs of love-sickness:
    (Polonius:) How now, Ophelia! What's the matter?
    (Ophelia:) Alas, my lord, I have been so affrighted!   (Alas only in F)
    (Polonius:) With what, i' the name of God?
    (Ophelia:) My lord, as I was sewing in my chamber,   (closet, Q2)
    Lord Hamlet . with his doublet all unbraced,
    No hat upon his head; his stockings fouled,
    Ungartered, and down-gyvèd to his ankle;   (like fetters)
    Pale as his shirt; his knees knocking each other;
    And with a look so piteous in purport
    As if he had been loosèd out of hell
    To speak of horrors – he comes before me
    (Polonius:) Mad for thy love?
    (Ophelia:)   My lord, I do not know;
    But truly I do fear it.
    (Polonius:)   What said he?
    (Ophelia:) He took me by the wrist, and held me hard;
    Then goes he to the length of all his arm,
    And with his other hand thus o'er his brow,
    He falls to such perusal of my face
    As he would draw it. Long stayed he so;
    At last – a little shaking of mine arm,
    And thrice his head thus waving up and down –
    He raised a sigh so piteous and profound
    That it did seem to shatter all his bulk

And end his being; that done he lets me go:
And, with his head over his shoulder turned,
He seemed to find his way without his eyes;
For out o' doors he went without their help,
And to the last bended their light on me.
(Polonius:) Come, go with me: I will go seek the king.
This is the very ecstasy of love.   (2.1.74)

But the sub-plot of love is sex, and it is never far away:
    (Queen Gertrude:) Come hither, my good Hamlet, sit by me.
                                                        (good - F, dear – Q2)
    (Hamlet:) No, good mother, here's metal more attractive.
    (Polonius, to the King:) O, ho! do you mark that?
    (Hamlet, lying down at Ophelia's feet:) Lady, shall I lie in your lap?
    (Ophelia:) No, my lord.
    (Hamlet:) I mean, my head upon your lap?
    (Ophelia:) Ay, my lord.
    (Hamlet:) Do you think I meant country matters?
    (Ophelia:) I think nothing, my lord.
    (Hamlet:) That's a fair thought to lie between maids' legs.
    (Ophelia:) What is, my lord?
    (Hamlet:) Nothing.
    (Ophelia:) You are merry, my lord.   (3.2.116)

Hamlet sends love-letters to Ophelia :
                    Doubt thou the stars are fire;
                Doubt that the sun doth move;
                    Doubt truth to be liar;
                But never doubt I love.
    O dear Ophelia, I am ill at these numbers,
    I have not art to reckon my groans: but that I
    love thee best, O most best, believe it. Adieu.
            Thine evermore, most dear lady, whilst this
            machine is to him,   HAMLET.   (2.2.115)

Then love changes to indifference, and worse, as Ophelia is spurned,
and hands his letters back to Hamlet:
    (Ophelia:) My lord, I have remembrances of yours,
    That I have longèd long to re-deliver;
    I pray you, now receive them.

46

(Hamlet:)   No, not I;
I never gave you aught.
(Ophelia:) My honoured lord, you know right well you did;
And, with them, words of so sweet breath composed
As made the things more rich: their perfume lost,
Take these again; for to the noble mind
Rich gifts wax poor when givers prove unkind.
There, my lord.   (3.1.93)

    Shakespeare frequently comments on the fickleness and inconstancy
of love:
Sigh no more, ladies, sigh no more,
        Men were deceivers ever,
One foot in sea and one on shore,
        To one thing constant never:
Then sigh not so, but let them go,
        And be you blithe and bonny,
Converting all your sounds of woe
        Into Hey nonny, nonny.   (MAAN 2.3.65)

... ...
If music be the food of love, play on,
Give me excess of it; that, surfeiting,
The appetite may sicken and so die -
That strain again – it had a dying fall;
O, it came o'er my ear like the sweet south,
That breathes upon a bank of violets,
Stealing, and giving odour.   – Enough; no more;
'Tis not so sweet now as it was before.
O spirit of love, how quick and fresh art thou!
That, not withstanding thy capacity
Receiveth as the sea, nought enters there,
Of what validity and pitch soe'er,
But falls into abatement and low price
Even in a minute! so full of shapes is fancy,
That it alone is high-fantastical.   (TN 1.1.1)

... ...
O, how this spring of love resembleth
The uncertain glory of an April day,
Which now shows all the beauty of the sun,
And by and by a cloud takes all away!

47

Even as one heat another heat expels,
Or as one nail by strength drives out another,
So the remembrance of my former love
Is by a newer object quite forgotten.   (TGV 1.3.84)

… … … … … … … … … …

The course of true love never did run smooth…
… if there were a sympathy in choice.   (mutual attraction)
War, death, or sickness did lay siege to it,
Making it momentary as a sound
Swift as a shadow, short as any dream,
Brief as the lightning in the collied night,   (=coal-black)
That, in a spleen, unfolds both heaven and earth,
And ere a man hath power to say, 'Behold!'
The jaws of darkness do devour it up;
So quick bright things come to confusion.   (MND 1.1.134)

… … … … … … … … … …

Antony, one of the triumvirate that ruled the Roman Empire, throws
it all away because of his infatuation with Cleopatra:
        Nay, but this dotage of our general's
        O'erflows the measure …
                                … his captain's heart
        Which in the scuffles of great fights hath burst
        The buckles on his breast, reneges all temper,   (unrestrained)
        And is become the bellows and the fan
        To cool a gipsy's lust. Look! where they come.
        Take but good note, and you shall see in him
        The triple pillar of the world transformed
        Into a strumpet's fool. Behold and see.
        (Cleopatra:) If it be love indeed, tell me how much.
        (Antony:) There's beggary in the love that can be reckoned…
        (Enter an attendant:) News, my good lord, from Rome. …
        … (Antony:) Let Rome in Tiber melt, and the wide arch
        Of the ranged empire fall! Here is my space.   (1.1.1)
Even betrothal to Octavius' sister does not end his obsession:
    -        Now Antony must leave her utterly.
    -        Never; he will not:
        Age cannot wither her, nor custom stale
        Her infinite variety; other women cloy
        The appetites they feed, but she makes hungry

Where most she satisfies. (2.2.241)

Shakespeare has plenty to say about sex as distinct from love. It is a curiously ambivalent design of nature on the one hand to favour a stable man-woman family as the best environment for the rearing of children, yet at the same time to endow those same men and women with a promiscuous sexual urge which is capable of blowing families apart. Here is Ulysses' opinion of Cressida:

Fie, fie upon her!
There's language in her eye, her cheeks, her lip,
Nay, her foot speaks: her wanton spirits look out
At every joint and motive of her body.
O, these encounterers, so glib of tongue,
That give accosting welcome ere it comes, (meeting half way)
And wide unclasp the tables of their thoughts (notebooks)
To every ticklish reader! set them down
For sluttish spoils of opportunity
And daughters of the game. (T&C 4.4.54)

And Thersites, in the same play:

Patroclus will give me anything for the intelligence of this whore: the parrot will not do more for an almond than he for a commodious drab. Lechery, lechery, still wars and lechery; nothing else holds fashion: a burning devil take them! (5.2.189)

… … … … … … … … … … … … …

Gloucester recognises the mad King Lear :

Is't not the king?
(Lear:)   Ay, every inch a king:
When I do stare, see how the subject quakes.
I pardon that man's life – What was thy cause? –
Adultery? –
Thou shalt not die: die for adultery! No:
The wren goes to't, and the small gilded fly
Does lecher in my sight.
Let copulation thrive; for Gloucester's bastard son
Was kinder to his father than my daughters
Got 'tween the lawful sheets.
To't luxury, pell-mell! for I lack soldiers. (luxury =lust)
Behold yond simpering dame,
Whose face between her forks presageth snow; (= legs)

49

That minces virtue, and does shake the head
To hear of pleasure's name;
The fitchew nor the soilèd horse goes to't   (f=polecat;whore)
With a more riotous appetite.
Down from the waist they are Centaurs,
Though women all above;
But to the girdle do the gods inherit,
Beneath is all the fiends':
There's hell, there's darkness, there is the sulphurous pit,
Burning, scalding, stench, consumption; fie, fie, fie!
pah,pah! Give me an ounce of civet, good apothecary, to
sweeten my imagination.   (civet=perfume from civet cat)

                                                        (4.6.109)

... ...
Love comforteth like sunshine after rain,
But lust's effect is tempest after sun;
Love's gentle spring doth always fresh remain,
Lust's winter comes ere summer half be done.
          Love surfeits not; lust like a glutton dies:
          Love is all truth, lust full of forgèd lies.   (V&A 799)

Shakespeare speaks of casual sex with disgust, and it is a reasonable
guess that his condemnation of it was based on personal experience. Long
absences from his Stratford wife combined with the natural appetite of a
virile man would have made opportunities for sexual encounters hard to
resist. Sonnet 129 expresses the shame following such an encounter:
          The expense of spirit in a waste of shame
          Is lust in action; and till action, lust
          Is perjured, murderous, bloody, full of blame,
          Savage, extreme, rude, cruel, not to trust;
          Enjoyed no sooner but despisèd straight;
          Past reason hunted; and no sooner had,
          Past reason hated, as a swallowed bait,
          On purpose laid to make the taker mad;
          Mad in pursuit, and in possession so;
          Had, having, and in quest to have, extreme;
          A bliss in proof, - and proved, a very woe;   (=tested)
          Before, a joy proposed; behind, a dream.
                    All this the world well knows; yet none knows well
                    To shun the heaven that leads men to this hell.

50

The best answer and antidote to that foul perversion of love is the noblest sonnet of them all;

> Let me not to the marriage of true minds
> Admit impediments. Love is not love
> Which alters when it alteration finds,
> Or bends with the remover to remove:
> O no; it is an ever fixèd mark,
> That looks on tempests, and is never shaken;
> It is the star to every wandering bark,
> Whose worth's unknown, although his height be taken.
> Love's not Time's fool, though rosy lips and cheeks
> Within his bending sickle's compass come;
> Love alters not with his brief hours and weeks,
> But bears it out even to the edge of doom.
> > If this be error, and upon me proved,
> > I never writ, nor no man ever loved.   (Son 116)

How strong was Shakespeare's own marriage? He was separated from his family for months at a time during his theatre years, for Aubrey wrote that 'He was wont to go to his native country once a year.' His marriage to Anne may well have been a 'shotgun wedding', a teenage folly to be repented at leisure, if we may so interpret various lines in All's Well That Ends Well, such as:

> (Bertram:) certain it is I liked her
> And boarded her in the wanton way of youth   (5.3.212)
> -
> > War is no strife
> To the dark house and the detested wife   (2.3.308)
> -
> A young man married is a man that's marred   (2.3.316)

But our guess is completely wrong, for these lines were written for the sake of a good plot which ends happily, as Bertram confesses:

> I'll love her dearly, ever dearly   (5.3.321)

An old sexton of Stratford asserted that Shakespeare's widow 'did earnestly desire to be laid in the same grave with him.' To me that is conclusive proof that the affection between them was lifelong.

And so we return to the celebration of that most powerful and joyous emotion that life offers us:

Here is Rosalind once more, with a couple of extracts:

> Nay, 'tis true: there was never anything so sudden but the fight of two rams, and Caesar's thrasonical brag of – I came, saw, and overcame: for your brother and my sister no sooner met, but they looked; no sooner looked, but they loved; no sooner loved, but they sighed; no sooner sighed, but they asked one another the reason; no sooner knew the reason, but they sought the remedy; and in these degrees have they made a pair of stairs to marriage, which they will climb incontinent, or else be incontinent before marriage: they are in the very wrath of love, and they will together: clubs cannot part them. (AYLI 5.2.33)

Here she urges shepherdess Phebe to say yes to Silvius:

> But mistress, know yourself. Down on your knees,
> And thank heaven, fasting, for a good man's love:
> For I must tell you friendly in your ear,
> Sell when you can, you are not for all markets.
> Cry the man mercy, love him, take his offer.   (3.5.57)

There is a strong bond of love in the best marriages, and this excerpt from Julius Caesar celebrates it:

> The scene is Brutus' house in the small hours of the morning.
> (Portia:)   Dear my lord,
> Make me acquainted with your cause of grief.
> (Brutus:) I am not well in health, and that is all.
> (Portia:) Brutus is wise, and were he not in health,
> He would embrace the means to come by it.
> (Brutus:) Why, so I do. Good Portia, go to bed.
> (Portia:) Is Brutus sick, and is it physical
> To walk unbraced and suck up the humours
> Of the dank morning? What, is Brutus sick,
> And will he steal out of his wholesome bed,
> To dare the vile contagion of the night,
> And tempt the rheumy and unpurgèd air
> To add unto his sickness? No, my Brutus!
> You have some sick offence within your mind,
> Which by the right and virtue of my place
> I ought to know of: and upon my knees,
> I charm you, by my once- commended beauty,
> By all your vows of love and that great vow

Which did incorporate and make us one,
That you unfold to me, yourself, your half,
Why you are so heavy, and what men tonight
Have had resort to you; for here have been
Some six or seven, who did hide their faces
Even from darkness.
(Brutus:)   Kneel not, gentle Portia,
(Portia:) I should not need, if you were gentle Brutus.
Within the bond of marriage, tell me, Brutus,
Is it excepted I should know no secrets
That appertain to you? Am I yourself
But, as it were, in sort or limitation,
To keep with you at meals, comfort your bed,
And talk to you sometimes? Dwell I but in the suburbs   (the brothel
Of your good pleasure? If it be no more,   areas)
Portia is Brutus' harlot, not his wife.
(Brutus:) You are my true and honourable wife,
As dear to me as are the ruddy drops
That visit my sad heart.
(Portia:) If this were true, then should I know this secret.
I grant I am a woman, but withal
A woman well-reputed, Cato's daughter.
Think you I am no stronger than my sex,
Being so fathered and so husbanded?
Tell me your counsels, I will not disclose 'em.
I have made strong proof of my constancy,
Giving myself a voluntary wound
Here in the thigh. Can I bear that with patience
And not my husband's secrets?
(Brutus:)   O, ye gods,
Render me worthy of this noble wife!   (2.1.255)
... ...

Shakespeare's treatment of love is so wide-ranging that many choice quotations will not fit into a small book, and have had to be omitted. In the case of Romeo and Juliet snippets from here and there will not do: the whole play must be read. Love at first sight has never been better described than in the scene in the Tempest where Ferdinand and Miranda meet, and the reader must seek that out.

The sonnets are all devoted to the theme of love, and it is tempting to quote many of them, but space will not allow it. I make exception however for the wry honesty and humour of Sonnet 130:

My mistress' eyes are nothing like the sun;
Coral is far more red than her lips' red,
If snow be white, why then her breasts are dun;
If hairs be wires, black wires grow on her head.
I have seen roses damask'd, red and white,
But no such roses see I in her cheeks;
And in some perfumes there is more delight
Than in the breath that from my mistress reeks.
I love to hear her speak, yet well I know
That music hath a far more pleasing sound;
I grant I never saw a goddess go, -
My mistress, when she walks, treads on the ground:
 And yet, by heaven, I think my love as rare
 As any she belied with false compare.

... ...

To close this chapter I append a mixed bag of one-line comments:
(Poins), pointing to Falstaff, who has Doll Tearsheet on his knee:
Is it not strange that desire should so many years outlive performance? (2 Hy IV 2.4.267)

... ...

Beauty provoketh fools sooner than gold. (AYLI 1.3.113)

... ...

To be wise, and love, exceeds man's might. (T&C 3.2.163)

... ...

Were man but constant, he were perfect. (TGV 5.4.110)

... ...

To say the truth, reason and love keep little company together nowadays. (MND 3.1.150)

... ...

Men have died from time to time, and worms have eaten them, but not for love. (AYLI 5.2.33)

... ...

(A note about the sonnets:)

There is no space in this short book in which to examine the complex and still mysterious story behind the sonnets. It will be sufficient to say that Shakespeare appears to have been asked to write some of the earlier ones in order to persuade a young man to marry. In the course of that the poet himself seemingly falls in love with the young man (the 'lovely boy', 'the master-mistress of my passion'). Beginning with Sonnet 127, there follows a sequence implying a sexual relationship between the youth and a lady who is also Shakespeare's mistress. Then a later series of sonnets are addressed to the lady herself, some of which express the poet's sense of shame and even disgust with his sexual relationship with this married woman. She is described as 'a woman coloured ill', and some scholars have identified this 'Dark lady' as Emilia Lanier, a member of a family of Venetian Jews, royal musicians, long resident in London in the guise of nominal Christians. That Emilia had a swarthy complexion is corroborated when we learn that two of her cousins were described in a court case as 'black men'.

This traumatic relationship with the mysterious temptress coincided with a change in Shakespeare's style. After 1600 the writing becomes darker, more cynical, more world-hating, more misogynistic, expressing revulsion against sex itself, especially in the great tragedies. The two final sonnets, variations of a single original, hint strongly at venereal disease derived from his affair, as we see here:

(Sonnet 153 refers to)

> ... a seething bath, which yet men prove
> Against strange maladies a sovereign cure ...
> ... I, sick withal, the help of bath desired   (the city?)
> And thither hied, a sad distempered guest,
> But found no cure ...

(And sonnet 154 refers to)

> ... a healthful remedy
> For men diseased.

We are entitled to guess that Shakespeare's change of writing style stemmed from the sexual guilt and self-condemnation of an honourable man who had broken his marriage vows with a married woman. During that same period he became obsessed with skin disease and other maladies. For example, in Troilus and Cressida, dating from 1601-2, we hear of:

The rotten diseases of the south, the guts-griping, ruptures, catarrhs, loads o'gravel i' th' back, lethargies, cold palsies, raw eyes, dirt-rotten livers, wheezing lungs, bladders full of imposthume, sciaticas, limekilns i' th' palm, incurable bone-ache, and the rivell'd fee-simple of the tetter. (skin eruption)

(T&C 5.1.21)

It is tempting to think that Shakespeare himself suffered from some similar disease during that time. Of course, such diseases may have had no sexual connection, but followed simply from the appalling diet of the period. Dr John Hall, Shakespeare's son-in-law, had to treat patients suffering from scurvy. Looking for dietary evidence in the plays, I counted over one hundred references to meat in its various forms, but hardly any references to fresh vegetables and fruit which would have prevented scurvy. There are 8 mentions of salad and one reference each to lettuce and cabbage, two each to lemons and oranges.

Then after the violent language of Timon of Athens, the sky suddenly clears, and Shakespeare puts all that trauma behind him and moves into a new era of mellow serenity, and in that mood he writes Antony & Cleopatra, at the top of his form. The word 'plague' is found 13 times in Timon, 8 times in Troilus and King Lear, but is absent from Antony and Cleopatra and the Winter's Tale.

COMEDY, WIT, and IRONY

Every age has its own humour. The long-winded captions to Punch cartoons that made Victorians laugh leave us mystified. Old music hall songs that entertained an earlier generation are merely museum pieces now. A good deal of Shakespeare's humour is best forgotten. He was a man of his time, and, following the fashion of the university wits, he was overfond of puns and other word-play, and that becomes tiresome to modern taste.

But when it comes to the portrayal of ridiculous characters, or pricking the bubble of pomposity, or seeing the comic side of confused or dangerous situations, Shakespeare is still a master of comedy. In Hamlet and the 'bitter comedies' he also introduces a wry, caustic humour, the truth of which still evokes an answering chord in us today. Exactly *why* we laugh at anything is always a mystery, and any attempt to analyse humour is the best way to kill it stone dead, for 'brevity is the soul of wit'. The extracts that follow are therefore offered without further comment, in the hope that at least some of it still has the power to entertain us.

Sir John Falstaff is the best-known comic character in the plays, and he appears to be an entirely original creation of Shakespeare's imagination. The plays that tell the story of Henry the Fourth and Fifth deal with historic themes of high seriousness, but our author knows that typical human behaviour is a mixture of seriousness and folly, and he likes to inject liberal doses of the latter. There is always to be found in us a measure of what used to be called the World, the Flesh and the Devil. For that reason Shakespeare calls into being Sir John as an antidote to sober morality. His character follows in the medieval tradition of the Lord of Misrule, and jesters and fools always played an important part in dramas and masques before Shakespeare's time.

After the death of the great warrior king, Henry Vth, the old chroniclers created the legend of his supposedly riotous youth, which, after he became king, was transformed into high seriousness and nobility of nature. For example, according to Fabyan's Chronicle of 1516:

> This man, before the death of his father, applied him unto all vice and insolency, and drew unto him all rioters and wild disposed

persons; but after he was admitted to the rule of the land, anon and suddenly he became a new man, and turned all that rage into soberness and wise sadness, and the vice into constant virtue.

Thus we see why wild Prince Hal, woven into a play, clearly needed dissolute companions, and so was created Sir John Falstaff.　(See the note at the end of the chapter.)

Let us eavesdrop on the two of them in their favourite tavern in Eastcheap. The news is that rebellion is afoot, and Hal will be summoned to court to play his part in quelling it. Sir John warns Hal he will have to face his father on the morrow, the implication being that he will be called to account for his dissolute life. Hal suggests that Falstaff plays the part of the king in such an inquisition, and then they will switch roles again so that the Prince now plays his own father, and the fat knight plays the part of Hal.

> (Fal:) Well, thou wilt be horribly chid tomorrow when thou comest to thy father: if thou love me, practise an answer.
> (Prince:) Do thou stand for my father, and examine me upon the particulars of my life.
> (Fal:) Shall I? content: this chair shall be my state, this dagger my sceptre, and this cushion my crown...
> ... And here is my speech. Stand aside, nobility.
> (Mistress Quickly, Hostess:) O Jesu! This is excellent sport, i' faith!
> (Fal:) Weep not, sweet queen, for trickling tears are vain.
> (Quick:) O, the father! how he holds his countenance.
> (Fal:) For God's sake, lords, convey my tristful queen, For tears do stop the flood-gates of her eyes.
> (Quick:) O Jesu! he doth it as like one of these harlotry players as ever I see!
> (Fal :) Peace, good pint-pot! peace, good tickle-brain! Harry, I do not only marvel where thou spendest thy time, but also how thou art accompanied: for though the camomile, the more it is trodden on, the faster it grows, yet youth, the more it is wasted, the sooner it wears. That thou art my son, I have partly thy mother's word, partly my own opinion; but chiefly a villainous trick of thine eye and a foolish hanging of thy nether lip, that doth warrant me... Shall the son of England prove a thief and take purses? a question to be asked. There is a thing, Harry, which thou hast often heard of, and it is known to many in our land by the name of pitch: this

pitch, as ancient writers do report, doth defile; so doth the company thou keepest... And yet there is a virtuous man whom I have often noted in thy company, but I know not his name.

(Prince:) What manner of man, an it like your majesty?

(Fal:) A goodly portly man, i' faith, and a corpulent; of a cheerful look, a pleasing eye, and a most noble carriage; and, as I think, his age some fifty, or by'r lady, inclining to threescore; and now I remember me, his name is Falstaff: if that man should be lewdly given, he deceiveth me; for, Harry, I see virtue in his looks... peremptorily I speak it, there is virtue in that Falstaff: him keep with, the rest banish. And tell me now, thou naughty varlet, tell me, where hast thou been this month?

(Prince:) Dost thou speak like a king? Do thou stand for me, and I'll play my father...

... Now, Harry! whence come you?

(Fal:) My noble lord , from Eastcheap.

(Prince:) The complaints I hear of thee are grievous.

(Fal:) 'Sblood, my lord, they are false...

(Prince:) ... Thou art violently carried away from grace: there is a devil haunts thee in the likeness of a fat old man; a tun (hogshead) of man is thy companion. Why dost thou converse with that trunk of humours, that bolting-hutch of beastliness, that swoll'n parcel of dropsies, that huge bombard of sack, (sack: sherry; Spanish seco, dry) stuffed cloak-bag of guts, that roasted Manningtree ox with the pudding in his belly, that reverend vice, that grey iniquity, that father ruffian, that vanity in years? Wherein is he good but to taste sack and drink it? wherein neat and cleanly but to carve a capon and eat it? wherein cunning but in craft? wherein crafty but in villainy? wherein villainous but in all things? wherein worthy but in nothing?

(Fal:) I would your grace would take me with you: whom means your grace?

(Prince:) That villainous abominable misleader of youth, Falstaff, that old white-bearded Satan.

(Fal:) My lord, the man I know. That he is old, the more the pity, his white hairs do witness it; but that he is, saving your reverence, a whoremaster, that I utterly deny. If sack and sugar be a fault, God help the wicked! If to be old and merry be a sin, then many an old host that I know is damned: if to be fat be to be hated, then Pharaoh's lean kine are to be loved. No, my good lord; banish

Peto, banish Bardolph, banish Poins; but for sweet Jack Falstaff, kind Jack Falstaff, true Jack Falstaff, valiant Jack Falstaff, and therefore more valiant, being, as he is, old Jack Falstaff, banish not him thy Harry's company: banish not him thy Harry's company: banish plump Jack, and banish all the world.

At that point Bardolph comes running in:
O! my lord, my lord, the sheriff with a most monstrous watch is at the door...
(Prince:) ... Go, hide thee behind the arras: the rest walk up above. Now, my masters, for a true face and good conscience.
(Fal:) Both which I have had; but their date is out, and therefore I'll hide me.

After the danger has passed, Peto discovers:
Falstaff! fast asleep behind the arras, and snorting like a horse.
(Prince:) Hark, how hard he fetches breath. Search his pockets. (he searcheth his pockets, and findeth certain papers) What hast thou found?
(Peto:) Nothing but papers, my lord.
(Prince:) Let's see what they be: read them.
(Peto:) "Item, A capon   2s,2d.
Item, Sauce   4d.
Item, Sack, two gallons   5s, 8d.
Item, Anchovies and sack after
                supper   2s, 6d.
Item, Bread   ½d."
(Prince:) O monstrous! But one half-pennyworth of bread to this intolerable deal of sack!   (1 Hy IV 2.4.414)

Periodically Falstaff has faint pangs of conscience about his dissolute life, and thinks of repentance, but not
for long.
(Fal:) Bardolph, am I not fallen away vilely since this last action? do I not bate? do I not dwindle? Why, my skin hangs about me like an old lady's loose gown; I am withered like an old apple-john. Well, I'll repent, and that suddenly, while I am in some liking; I shall be out of heart shortly, and then I shall have no strength to repent. An I have forgotten what the inside of a church is made of, I am a peppercorn, a brewer's horse: the inside

of a church! Company, villainous company, hath been the spoil of me.

(Bardolph:) Sir John, you are so fretful, you cannot live long.

(Falstaff:) Why, there it is: come, sing me a bawdy song; make me merry. I was as virtuously given as a gentleman need to be; virtuous enough; swore little; diced not above seven times a week; went to a bawdy–house not above once in a quarter – of an hour; paid money that I borrowed – three or four times: lived well, and in good compass: and now I live out of all order, out of all compass. (1 Hy IV 3.3.1)

In The Merry Wives of Windsor he is once more inclined to repentance:

...if my wind were but long enough to say my prayers, I would repent. (4.5.106)

Falstaff is always an imaginative liar:

(Fal:) as the devil would have it, three misbegotten knaves in Kendal green came at my back and let drive at me; - for it was so dark, Hal, that thou couldst not see thy hand.

(Prince:) These lies are like the father that begets them – gross as a mountain, open, palpable. Why, thou clay-brained guts, thou knotty-pated fool, thou whoreson, obscene, greasy tallow-keech–

(Fal:) What, art thou mad? art thou mad? is not the truth the truth?

(Prince:) Why, how couldst thou know these men in Kendal green, when it was so dark thou couldst not see thy hand? Come, tell us your reason: what sayest thou to this?

(Poins:) Come, your reason, Jack, your reason.

(Fal:) What, upon compulsion? Zounds, and I were at the strappado, or all the racks in the world, I would not tell you on compulsion. Give a reason on compulsion? If reasons were as plentiful as blackberries, I would give no man a reason on compulsion, I. (1 Hy IV 2.4.249)

(strappado = torture involving suspension from rope)

Falstaff is apprehensive before the battle of Shrewsbury:

(Fal:) I would 'twere bedtime, Hal, and all well.

(Prince:) Why, thou owest God a death. (Exit)

(Fal:) 'Tis not due yet: I would be loath to pay him before his day. What need I be so forward with him that calls not on me? Well, 'tis no matter; honour pricks me on. Yea, but how if honour prick me off when I come on? How then? Can honour set to a leg? No. Or an arm? No. Or take away the grief of a wound? No. Honour hath no skill in surgery then? No. What is honour? A word. What is in that word honour? What is that honour? Air. A trim reckoning! Who hath it? He that died o' Wednesday, Doth he feel it? No. Doth he hear it? No. 'Tis insensible then? Yea, to the dead. But will it not live with the living? No. Why? Detraction will not suffer it. Therefore I'll none of it. Honour is a mere scutcheon – and so ends my catechism. (5.1.126)

(scutcheon = coat of arms honouring the dead)

At the height of the tempest which gives its name to the play, shipwreck and death seem imminent, but Shakespeare still manages to inject some humour into the situation. The boatswain urges the passengers to go below and get out of the way of the sailors.

(Boats:) You mar our labour; keep your cabins: you do assist the storm.

(Gonzalo:) Nay, good, be patient.

(Boats:) When the sea is. Hence! What care these roarers for the name of king? To cabin: silence! trouble us not.

(Gon:) Good; yet remember whom thou hast aboard.

(Boats:) None that I more love than myself … Out of our way, I say.

(Gonzalo:) I have great comfort from this fellow: methinks he hath no drowning mark upon him; his complexion is perfect gallows. Stand fast, good fate, to his hanging! Make the rope of his destiny our cable, for our own doth little advantage! If he be not born to be hanged, our case is miserable. … Now would I give a thousand furlongs of sea for an acre of barren ground – long heath, brown furze, anything. (1.1.14)

While we have that play in mind, here are more good lines:

- He receives comfort like cold porridge. (2.1.10)

- Look, he's winding up the watch of his wit; by and by it will strike. (2.1.12)

- Prithee, do not turn me about: my stomach is not constant.

  (2.2.115)

- They say there's but five upon this isle: we are three of them; if th'other two be brained like us, the state totters. (3.2.5)

In Much Ado About Nothing Shakespeare has created Dogberry, a caricature of an ignorant constable, assisted by his even more incompetent night watchmen:

- (Dogberry:) First, who think you the most desertless man to be constable?

- (First Watch:) Hugh Oatcake, sir, or George Seacoal; for they can write and read.

- (Dogb:) Come hither, neighbour Seacoal. God hath blessed you with a good name: to be a well-favoured man is the gift of fortune; but to write and read comes by nature.

- (Second Watch:) Both which, Master constable –

- (Dogb:) You have: I knew it would be your answer. Well, for your favour, sir, why, give God thanks, and make no boast of it; and for your writing and reading, let that appear when there is no need of such vanity. You are thought here to be the most senseless and fit man for the constable of the watch; therefore bear you the lantern. This is your charge: you shall comprehend all vagrom men; you are to bid any man stand, in the prince's name.

- (2 Watch:) How, if a' will not stand?

- (Dogb:) Why, then, take no note of him, but let him go; and presently call the rest of the watch together, and thank God you are rid of a knave.

- (Verges:) If he will not stand when he is bidden, he is none of the prince's subjects.

- (Dogb:) True, and they are to meddle with none but the prince's subjects. ...

63

- ... Well, you are to call at all the alehouses, and bid them that are drunk get them to bed.

- (2 Watch:) How if they will not?

- (Dogb:) Why, then, let them alone till they are sober...

- ... if you meet a thief, you may suspect him, by virtue of your office, to be no true man: and, for such kind of men, the less you meddle or make with them, why, the more is for your honesty.

- (2 Watch:) If we know him to be a thief, shall we not lay hands on him?

- (Dogb:) Truly, by your office you may; but I think they that touch pitch will be defiled: the most peaceable way for you, if you do take a thief, is to let him show himself what he is, and steal out of your company.

- (Verges:) You have been always called a merciful man, partner.

- (Dogb:) Truly, I would not hang a dog by my will, much more a man who hath any honesty in him .. (2 Watch:) Well, masters, we hear our charge: let us go sit here upon the church-bench till two, and then all go to bed. (3.3.9)

Dogberry invented malapropisms long before Mrs Malaprop:
 (Dogb:) One word, sir: our watch, sir, have indeed compre-hended two auspicious persons, and we would have them this morning examined before your worship.
 (Leonato:) Take their examination yourself, and bring it me; I am now in great haste, as it may appear unto you. (3.5.49)
 ... ...
 (Dogb:) Is our whole dissembly appeared?
 (Verges:) O, a stool and a cushion for the sexton!
 (Sexton:) Which be the malefactors?
 (Dogb:) Marry, that am I and my partner.
 (Verges:) Nay, that's certain; we have the exhibition to examine.
 (Sexton:) But which are the offenders that are to be examined? let them come before master constable.

(Dogb:) Yes, marry, let them come before me. – What is your name, friend?

(Borachio:) Borachio.

(Dogb:) Pray write down – Borachio. - Yours, sirrah?

(Conrade:) I am a gentleman, sir, and my name is Conrade.

(Dogb:) Write down – master gentleman Conrade. - Masters, do you serve God?

(Conrade & Borachio:) Yes , sir, we hope.

(Dogb:) Write down – that they hope they serve God: - and write God first; for God defend but God should go before such villains! - Masters, it is proved already that you are little better than false knaves; and it will go near to be thought so shortly. How answer you for yourselves?

(Conrade:) Marry, sir, we say we are none...

(Dogb:) Have you writ down – that they are none?

(Sexton:) Master constable, you go not the way to examine; you must call forth the Watch that are their accusers.

(Dogb:) Yes, marry, that's the eftest way. - Let the Watch come forth. - Masters, I charge you in the prince's name, accuse these men.

(First Watch:) This man said, sir, that Don John, the prince's brother was a villain.

(Dogb:) Write down - Prince John a villain. - Why, this is flat perjury, to call a prince's brother villain.

(Borachio:) Master constable, -

(Dogb:) Pray thee, fellow, peace; I do not like thy look, I promise thee.

(Sexton:) What heard you him say else?

(2nd Watch:) Marry, that he had received a thousand ducats off Don John for accusing the Lady Hero wrongfully.

(Dogb:) Flat burglary as ever was committed.

(Verges:) Yea, by the mass, that it is.

(Sexton:) What else, fellow?

(1st Watch:) And that Count Claudio did mean, upon his words, to disgrace Hero before the whole assembly, and not marry her.

(Dogb:) O villain! thou wilt be condemned into everlasting re-demption for this.

(Sexton:) What else?

(2nd Watch:) This is all. (4.2.1)

... ...

(Don Pedro:) Officers, what offence hath these men done?
(Dogb:) Marry, sir, they have committed false report; moreover,
they have spoken untruths; secondarily, they are slanders; sixth
and lastly, they have belied a lady; thirdly, they have verified unjust things: and, to conclude, they are lying knaves.   (5.1.208)

A passage in Aubrey's Brief Lives asserts that Shakespeare based the
character of Dogberry on a real-life constable: 'The Humour of the Constable in Midsomernight's Dreame (sic), he happened to take at Grendon,
in Bucks (I think it was Midsomer night that he happened to lye there)
which is the roade from London to Stratford, and there was living that
Constable about 1642, when I first came to Oxon. Ben Johnson and he did
gather Humours of men dayly where ever they came.'

In a Midsummer Night's Dream Shakespeare introduces the splendid and entertaining character of Nick Bottom the Weaver, a swash-
buckling extrovert, 'most ignorant of what he's most assured', a type of
loudmouth self-confident egotist known to us all. He is, of course, the
dominant member of that group of 'hard-handed men, that work in Athens here, which never laboured in their minds till now'. And what wonderful names they have: Peter Quince, the Carpenter; Snug, the Joiner;
Francis Flute, the Bellows-mender; Tom Snout, the Tinker; and Robert
Starveling, the Tailor. The 'play within a play', in which the 'rude me-
chanicals' decide that everything has to be explained to the audience,
must have drawn laughter because it is the very opposite of true acting.
Here are some extracts:

(Quince:) Here is the scroll of every man's name, which is thought
fit, through all Athens, to play in our interlude before the Duke
and Duchess, on his wedding-day at night.
(Bottom:) First, good Peter Quince, say what the play treats on;
then read the names of the actors, and so grow to a point.
(Quince:) Marry, our play is, The most lamentable comedy, and
most cruel death of Pyramus and Thisbe.
(Bottom:) A very good piece of work, I assure you, and a mer-
ry. Now, good Peter Quince, call forth   your actors by the scroll.
Masters, spread yourselves.
(Quince:) Answer as I call you. Nick Bottom, the weaver.
(Bottom:) Ready. Name what part I am for, and proceed.
(Quince:) You, Nick Bottom, are set down for Pyramus.
(Bottom:) What is Pyramus? A lover, or a tyrant?
(Quince:) A lover, that kills himself most gallantly for love.

(Bottom:) That will ask some tears in the true performing of it: if I do it, let the audience look to their eyes; I will move storms, I will condole in some measure. To the rest: yet my chief humour is for a tyrant. I could play Ercles rarely, or a part to tear a cat in, to make all split.

> The raging rocks
> And shivering shocks
> Shall break the locks
>   Of prison gates:
> And Phibbus' car   (chariot of Phoebus, the sun)
> Shall shine from far
> And make and mar
>   The foolish Fates   .

This was lofty! Now, name the rest of the players...

(Quince:) Francis Flute, the bellows-mender.

(Flute:) Here, Peter Quince.

(Quince:) You must take Thisbe on you.

(Flute:) What is Thisbe? a wandering knight?

(Quince:) It is the lady that Pyramus must love.

(Flute:) Nay, faith, let me not play a woman; I have a beard coming.

(Quince:) That's all one: you shall play it in a mask, and you may speak as small as you will.

(Bottom:) An I may hide my face, let me play Thisbe too. I'll speak in a monstrous little voice, 'Thisne, Thisne!' 'Ah Pyramus, my lover dear; thy Thisbe dear, and lady dear!'

(Quince:) No, no; you must play Pyramus; and Flute, you Thisbe...

... Snug, the joiner, you the lion's part.

(Snug:) Have you the lion's part written? pray you, if it be, give it me, for I am slow of study.

(Quince:) You may do it extempore, for it is nothing but roaring.

(Bottom:) Let me play the lion too. I will roar, that I will do any man's heart good to hear me; I will roar, that I will make the duke say, 'Let him roar again, let him roar again.'

(Quince:) An you should do it too terribly, you would fright the duchess and the ladies, that they would shriek; and that were enough to hang us all ...

(Bottom:) ... I will aggravate my voice so that I will roar you as

gently as any sucking dove; I will roar you as 'twere any nightingale.

(Quince:) You can play no part but Pyramus; for Pyramus is a sweet-faced man; a proper man, as one shall see in a summer's day; a most lovely gentleman-like man: therefore you must needs play Pyramus.   (1.2.4)

When the play is performed, Quince reads a Prologue, but is all at sea with the punctuation:

If we offend, it is with our good will.
That you should think, we come not to offend,
But with good will. To show our simple skill,
That is the true beginning of our end.
Consider then we come but in despite.
We do not come, as minding to content you,
Our true intent is. All for your delight,
We are not here. That you should here repent you,
The actors are at hand; and by their show,
You shall know all that you are like to know.   (5.1.108)

No doubt the actor who played Nick Bottom enjoyed 'hamming it up' as a parody of the bombastic style of less-skilled players in rival companies, and Shakespeare provided him with plenty of appalling lines to work on:

… with blade, with bloody, blameful blade,
He bravely broach'd his boiling bloody breast.
… … … … … … …
Sweet moon, I thank thee for thy sunny beams;
I thank thee, moon, for shining now so bright,
For, by thy gracious, golden, glittering gleams,
I trust to taste of truest Thisbe's sight…   (5.1.147)

Hippolyta complains that 'This is the silliest stuff that ever I heard,' to which Theseus replies: 'The best in this kind are but shadows, and the worst are no worse, if imagination amend them.'
… … … … … … … … … … …
Humorous lines are scattered throughout the plays:

- I had rather have a fool to make me merry than experience to make me sad.   (AYLI 4.1.28)

68

- Shall I lose my doctor? No, he gives me the potions and the motions. (MWW 3.1.93)

- This cannot be but a great courtier … a great man, I'll warrant: I know by the picking on's teeth. (WT 4.4.749)

- Remuneration! O! that's the Latin word for three farthings. (LLL 3.1.143)

- Thou speakest wiser than thou art 'ware of. (AYLI 2.4.57)
(Touchstone:) Nay, I shall ne'er be 'ware of mine own wit till I break my shins against it.

- (Mistress Quickly:) She is given too much to allicholy and musing. (MWW 1.4.147)

… … … … … … … … … …

Somewhere about 1600, after Shakespeare had created the cheerful and light-hearted As You Like It, the sun seems to have gone behind a cloud, as he entered a more serious world and greater depths of imagination, leading to the 'Bitter Comedies' and the great tragedies. Thus we find that the humour in Hamlet is caustic, even cruel. (see the note at the end of the chapter)

(Polonius:) What do you read, my lord? (2.2.195)
(Hamlet:) Words, words, words.
(Polonius:) What is the matter, my lord?
(Hamlet:) Between who?
(Polonius:) I mean the matter that you read, my lord.
(Hamlet:) Slanders, sir. For the satirical rogue says here that old men have grey beards, that their faces are wrinkled, their eyes purging thick amber and plum-tree gum, and that they have a plentiful lack of wit, together with most weak hams – all which, sir, though I most powerfully and potently believe, yet I hold it not honesty to have it thus set down. For yourself, sir, shall grow old as I am – if like a crab you could go backward.
(Polonius, aside:) Though this be madness, yet there is method in't – Will you walk out of the air, my lord?
(Hamlet:) Into my grave?
(Polonius:) Indeed, that's out of the air. (aside-) How pregnant

sometimes his replies are – a happiness that often madness hits on, which reason and sanity could not so prosperously be delivered of …

… My lord, I will take my leave of you.

(Hamlet:) You cannot, sir, take from me anything that I will not more willingly part withal – except my life, except my life, except my life.

(Polonius:) Fare you well , my lord.

(Hamlet:) These tedious old fools!

Soon after that, the arrival of the travelling players is announced, and Polonius describes them as:

The best actors in the world, either for tragedy, comedy, history, pastoral, pastoral-comical, historical-pastoral, tragical-historical, tragical-comical-historical-pastoral, scene individable, or poem unlimited.   (2.2.392)

Hamlet seems to regard obtuse Polonius as fair-game for a jest:

(Polonius:) My lord, the Queen would speak with you, and presently.

(Hamlet:) Do you see yonder cloud that's almost in shape of a camel?

(Polonius:) By th'mass and 'tis – like a camel indeed.

(Hamlet:) Methinks it is like a weasel.

(Polonius:) It is backed like a weasel.

(Hamlet:) Or like a whale?

(Polonius:) Very like a whale.

(Hamlet:) Then I will come to my mother by and by.

(aside:) They fool me to the top of my bent.   (= to the utmost limit)
                                                        (3.2.399)

Those who admire the nobility in the character of Hamlet find it difficult to come to terms with his indifference when he slays Polonius by chance, and the dismissive, wry humour with which he refers to the corpse. But the greatness of Shakespeare's creative imagination is demonstrated when he calls into being rounded human personalities, warts and all, whose behaviour is often irrational and wayward, and that no doubt applies to every one of us.

(King:) Now, Hamlet, where's Polonius?

(Hamlet:) At supper.

(King:) At supper? Where?

(Hamlet:) Not where he eats, but where he is eaten. A certain

70

convocation of politic worms are e'en at him. Your worm is your only emperor for diet: we fat all creatures else to fat us, and we fat ourselves for maggots. Your fat king and your lean beggar is but variable service – two dishes, but to one table. That's the end.
(King:) Alas, alas.
(Hamlet:) A man may fish with the worm that hath eat of a king, and eat of the fish that hath fed of that worm.
(King:) What dost thou mean by this?
(Hamlet:) Nothing but to show you how a king may go a progress through the guts of a beggar.
(King:) Where is Polonius?
(Hamlet:) In heaven. Send thither to see. If your messenger find him not there, seek him i'th'other place yourself. But if indeed you find him not within this month, you shall nose him as you go up the stairs into the lobby.   (4.3.17)

Macbeth is about murder, and the atmosphere of the play is sombre, to say the least. 'Blood' is mentioned 34 times. The audience need relief, and they get it in the form of the porter's jests. Coleridge, who normally has such a penetrating understanding of Shakespeare, cannot believe that he wrote the porter's lines: "This low soliloquy of the Porter and his few speeches afterwards, I believe to have been written for the mob by some other hand, perhaps with Shakespeare's consent... not one syllable has the ever-present being of Shakespeare." But most people would feel that this earthy humour has a part to play in defusing the almost unbearable tension felt by the audience as the action develops.

(Macduff:) Was it so late, friend, ere you went to bed, That you do lie so late?
(Porter:) Faith, sir, we were carousing till the second cock; and drink, sir, is a great provoker of three things.
(Macduff:) What three things does drink especially provoke?
(Porter:) Marry, sir, nose-painting, sleep, and urine. Lechery, sir, it provokes, and unprovokes; it provokes the desire, but it takes away the performance. Therefore much drink may be said to be an equivocator with lechery; it makes him, and it mars him; it sets him on, and it takes him off; it persuades him, and disheartens him; makes him stand to, and not stand to; in conclusion, equivocates him in a sleep, and giving him the lie, leaves him.   (2.3.25)

p. 45 A note on the origin of Sir John Falstaff:

The name Shakespeare first chose for this character was Sir John Old-castle. A person of that name lived between 1378 and 1417, was High Sheriff of Herefordshire, and became Lord Cobham on his marriage in 1409. He had indeed been a friend of Prince Hal, and campaigned with him in Wales against the Glyndŵr uprising. One chronicler wrote that 'his youth was full of wanton wildness before he knew the scriptures'. He became a Lollard, a follower of Wycliff, and for that reason King Henry, always an orthodox believer, broke with him and had him imprisoned in the Tower of London. From there he escaped and tried to organise a coup d'état, and when that failed he fled into hiding for four years, He was eventually captured, and on Christmas Day 1417 was hanged in chains and then roasted alive, 'dying without a cry' according to witnesses.

There was a late 16th Century play called 'The Famous Victories of Henry Vth' in which Sir John was portrayed as the boon companion of wild Prince Hal, and Shakespeare adopted that character and built upon it. When the plays about Henry IVth were staged, there was a protest from Oldcastle's descendant Sir Henry Brooke, later Lord Cobham, and Shakespeare seems to have changed the name at once, but so hastily that references to Oldcastle remain in the text, such as 'my old lad of the castle', and in the Prologue to Part 2: 'Our humble author will continue the story with Sir John in it … where for anything I know, Falstaff shall die of a sweat, unless already 'a be killed with your hard opinions for Oldcastle died martyr, and this is not the man.'

The name Falstaff was adapted from that of Sir John Fastolf, a warrior who fought at Agincourt, but who was accused of cowardice after retreating at the Battle of Patay. Although he was cleared of the charge, the accusation stuck to him.

p. 52 The change in Shakespeare's style from broad comedy to bitter humour coincided with a change of actor to play those parts. The clown Will Kemp who had played with much acclaim such parts as Lancelot Gobbo and Dogberry, left the company in 1600, and Shakespeare appointed in his place Robert Armin, whose temperament was more suited to the caustic wit of the roles written for him, such as Touchstone in As You Like It and the Fool in King Lear.

The names Gobbo and Dogberry demonstrate Shakespeare's love of inventing comic names for his comic characters. A list would include Sir Toby Belch, Sir Andrew Aguecheek, Mouldy, Wart, Mugs, Feeble, Fang, Shallow, Simple, Froth, Squeal, Thump, Pickbone, Oatcake and Dull.

And we have those ladies of easy virtue with their suggestive names: Mistress Quickly (pronounced quick-lie), Doll Tearsheet, Mistress Over-done and Jane Nightwork.

PATRIOTISM & WAR

Then a soldier,
Full of strange oaths, and bearded like the pard,
Jealous in honour, sudden and quick in quarrel,
Seeking the bubble reputation
Even in the cannon's mouth.

(AYLI 2.7.149)

Shakespeare grew up in an age inspired by patriotism. The nation ruled by Queen Elizabeth, Gloriana, had triumphed over powerful enemies. There was pride also in the bold adventurers such as Drake who sailed round the world, and earlier 'singed the King of Spain's beard' at Cadiz in 1587. After that date the two nations were unofficially at war until 1604. Richard Hakluyt, in his 'Voyages' of 1589, captures the enthusiasm of that time:

> Which of the Kings of this land before her Majesty, had their banners ever seen in the Caspian sea? Which of them hath ever dealt with the Emperor of Persia... ?... Who ever found English Consuls and Agents at Tripoli in Syria, at Aleppo, at Babylon, at Bakara, and, which is more, who ever heard of Englishmen at Goa before now? What English ship did heretofore ever anchor in the mighty river of Plate? Pass and repass the unpassable (in former opinion) strait of Magellan. . traverse the mighty breadth of the South Sea ... traffic with the Princes of Malaccas, and the isle of Java, double the famous Cape of Bona Speranza ... and last of all return home richly laden with the commodities of China, as the subjects of this now flourishing monarch have done?

The English language, via the pens of many gifted writers, expanded and blossomed, to do justice to the bold optimism of the age, and then came Shakespeare to crown the achievement through the plays. War is a central theme in those of his plays which are based on history, whether of England, or of Rome and Greece. Even though the plays which follow the course of the Wars of the Roses described events which took place a couple of centuries earlier, their spirit matches the patriotic mood of Elizabeth's reign, in which warfare is invested with noble virtues, such as honour, courage, and self-sacrifice. The atmosphere of the panoply of such welfare is conveyed in the words of Othello:

> Farewell the plumèd troop and the big wars
> That make ambition virtue! O, farewell!
> Farewell the neighing steed, and the shrill trump,
> The spirit-stirring drum, the ear-piercing fife,
> The royal banner, and all quality,
> Pride, pomp, and circumstance of glorious war!   (3.3.347)

How often many a good lad has been spellbound by the excitement of martial music, marched off to join the colours, only to end face-down in the reality of mud and blood. I am reminded of Wilfred Owen's poem, The Send-off:

> Down the close, darkening lanes they sang their way
> To the siding-shed,
> And lined the train with faces grimly gay.
> Their breasts were stuck all white with wreath and spray...
> ... Shall they return to beatings of great bells
> In wild trainloads?
> A few, a few, too few for drums and yells,
> May creep back, silent, to still village wells
> Up half-known roads.

The seamier side of battle tends to be absent from the plays, for it is highly unlikely that Shakespeare had any personal experience of war. Using the description of fighting recorded in the chronicles, he applied his imagination to create a credible picture of what war was like. He is bound to have heard first-hand accounts of warfare, especially from his patron and friend Henry Wriothesley, better known as the 3rd Earl of Southampton, who in 1596 and 1597 had accompanied the Earl of Essex on military expeditions to Cadiz and the Azores. In 1599 Southampton was appointed to high command in Essex's ill-fated campaign in Ireland. Later in his career he also saw military service in Germany.

The question may be asked whether Shakespeare's portrayal of the wars of that age has any relevance for us today, after mankind has suffered in two fearsome world wars which affected civilians in equal measure with soldiers, and in which were deployed high explosives, poison gas, flame-throwers and aerial bombardment undreamed of by Elizabethan commanders. And now we all live under the threat of weapons of mass destruction, perhaps wielded by individuals rather than by national armies.

On the other hand, the cause of all conflict lies within human nature, and that, unfortunately, has not changed during the long history of mankind. Therefore anything Shakespeare has to say about war, such as the motives that lead to it, chivalry towards opponents and compassion towards its victims should still carry weight for our present generation.

Of course he was the first to admit that it is impossible to represent warfare adequately upon a stage, as he explains in the Chorus which opens Henry the Fifth:

> O! for a Muse of fire, that would ascend
> The brightest heaven of invention;
> A kingdom for a stage, princes to act
> And monarchs to behold the swelling scene!
> Then should the war-like Harry, like himself,
> Assume the port of Mars; and at his heels,   (bearing of Mars)
> Leash'd in like hounds, should famine, sword, and fire
> Crouch for employment. But pardon, gentles all,
> The flat unraisèd spirits that hath dared
> On this unworthy scaffold to bring forth
> So great an object: can this cockpit hold
> The vasty fields of France? Or may we cram
> Within this wooden O the very casques
> That did affright the air at Agincourt?   (Prol.)

The 'wooden O' was probably the Curtain Theatre: the Globe was still under construction.

In the early performance of Henry Vth it is very likely that the actor who spoke the choruses was Shakespeare himself, if we judge by the words of the final Chorus:

> Thus far, with rough and all-unable pen,
>   Our bending author hath pursu'd the story;
> In little room confining mighty men,
>   Mangling by starts the full course of their glory... (Epilogue)

How do wars begin? Biologists, psychiatrists and anthropologists would tell us that aggression is a natural instinct to protect one's family and one's group from the aggression of neighbours. It is largely a male phenomenon: men are 26 times more likely to kill than are women. The medieval concept of courtly love required valiant knights to protect fair damsels, 'the weaker sex'. That there is a sexual undercurrent to all this cannot be avoided. For example, there is evidence that women prefer to mate with taller and stronger men, who are likely to father stronger children, hence the plumed helmets to make a warrior look even more powerful. It is easy to foment a feeling of loyalty to one's group, and hostility towards another group. This may be seen in house-competitions in boarding schools, inter-school games, and the whole world of football is a sublimation of aggression, in the rivalry of club versus club, nation versus nation.

The tendency of young men 'greatly to find quarrel in a straw' is seen in Romeo and Juliet, where

> Two households, both alike in dignity,
> > In fair Verona, where we lay our scene,
> From ancient grudge break to new mutiny,
> > Where civil blood makes civil hands unclean.   (Prol.)

Benvolio and Mercutio, friends of Romeo, walk in the streets:
(Ben:) I pray thee, good Mercutio, let's retire: the day is hot, the Capulets abroad, and, if we meet, we shall not 'scape a brawl; for now, these hot days, is the mad blood stirring.
(Mer:) Thou art like one of those fellows that, when he enters the confines of a tavern, claps me his sword upon the table, and says, 'God send me no need of thee!' and by the operation of the second cup draws it on the drawer, when, indeed, there is no need.

(drawer=tapster)

(Ben:) Am I like such a fellow?
(Mer:) Come, come, thou art as hot a Jack in thy mood as any in Italy; and as soon moved to be moody, and as soon moody to be moved.
(Ben:) And what to?
(Mer:) Nay, an there were two such, we should have none shortly, for one would kill the other. Thou! why, thou wilt quarrel with a man that hath a hair more or a hair less in his beard than thou hast. Thou wilt quarrel with a man for cracking nuts, having no other reason but because thou hast hazel eyes... Thou hast quarrelled with a man for coughing in the street, because he hath wakened thy dog that hath lain asleep in the sun. Didst thou not fall out with a tailor for wearing his new doublet before Easter? with another , for tying his new shoes with old riband?   (3.1.1)

There is a tradition that Shakespeare played the part of Benvolio. Earlier in the play the two sides taunt each other in the street, hoping for a brawl, a scene similar to the confrontation between urban gangs today.

> (Gregory:) Draw thy tool; here comes two of the house of Montagues.
> (Sampson:) My naked weapon is out: quarrel, I will back thee...
> (Gregory:) ... I will frown as I pass by; and let them take it as they list.
> (Sam:) Nay, as they dare. I will bite my thumb at them; which is a disgrace to them if they bear it.
> (Enter Abraham and Balthasar)
> (Abr:) Do you bite your thumb at us, sir?
> (Sam:) I do bite my thumb, sir...
> (Greg:) ... Do you quarrel, sir?   (1.1.36)

Very soon a fight starts with many more joining in. This type of blood-feud is war in miniature, still found thriving in remote areas of the world.

The Edict of Lyons, 501, declared that God directs the course of wars and even of private quarrels, so that the outcome of battles and duels may be taken as fair trial of right and justice. In 858 the Pope himself accepted that a duel was a 'just and legitimate combat,' and the practice of duelling spread across Europe, and was common in the Elizabethan Age. In France between 1601 and 1609, 2000 noblemen were killed in duels. Richard the Second opens with challenges to combat between Henry Bolingbroke ('Pale trembling coward, there I throw my gage') and Thomas Mowbray, Duke of Norfolk. Unfortunately, the attitude that God backs the winning side was still current in Shakespeare's day. In Henry Vth the King prays:

> O God of battles! Steel my soldiers' hearts...

In Hamlet, Shakespeare seems to take a more cynical view of war:

> (Hamlet:) Good sir, whose powers are these?
> (Captain:) They are of Norway, sir.
> (Ham:) How purpos'd, sir, I pray you?
> (Cap:) Against some part of Poland.
> (Ham:) Who commands them, sir?
> (Cap:) The nephew to old Norway, Fortinbras.
> (Ham:) Goes it against the main of Poland, sir,
>   Or for some frontier?
> (Cap:) Truly to speak, and with no addition,
> We go to gain a little patch of ground

That hath in it no profit but the name.
To pay five ducats – five – I would not farm it;
Nor will it yield to Norway or the Pole
A ranker rate should it be sold in fee   (ranker=higher)
(Ham:) Why, then the Polack never will defend it.
(Cap:) Yes, it is already garrison'd.
(Ham:) Two thousand souls and twenty thousand ducats
Will not debate the question of this straw!
This is th'impostume of much wealth and peace,   (imp=abscess)
That inward breaks, and shows no cause without
Why the man dies.   (4.4.9)

When the others have left, Hamlet continues to ponder the issues further (I omit the sentences where he relates it to his own predicament):
Witness this army, of such mass and charge,
Led by a delicate and tender prince,
Whose spirit, with divine ambition puff'd,
Makes mouths at the invisible event,   (scorning the outcome)
Exposing what is mortal and unsure
To all that fortune, death, and danger dare,
Even for an eggshell. Rightly to be great
Is not to stir without great argument,
But greatly to find quarrel in a straw
When honour's at the stake...
                        ... I see
The imminent death of twenty thousand men
That, for a fantasy and trick of fame,
Go to their graves like beds, fight for a plot
Whereon the numbers cannot try the cause,
Which is not tomb enough and continent
To hide the slain?   (4.4.47)

There is an ambiguity here: 'not to stir without great argument' is a policy to be warmly applauded, but such 'great argument' would surely rule out a 'straw', a word which emphasizes the triviality of the issue concerned. Ambition, and that dangerous word 'honour' seem to be the only motives for this and many another war. A prime cause of the wars of the 16th and 17th Centuries was religion, with its political corollary that princes in the northern half of Europe wanted to be break free from the constraining influence of the church of Rome and its allies, in the shape of Spain under Philip the Second and Austria under the Habsburgs. This might be summed up as a rise in nationalism, seen especially in the Dutch Republic, Denmark, Sweden and England itself, whose patriotism finds supreme expression in Shakespeare, with examples later in this chapter. Another motive for war in later centuries was trade, raw materials and markets, but that was not a dominant theme in the late Tudor age.

The Trojan War is semi-mythical, but the cause of it is the age-old cause of many a tribal conflict in primitive societies:

> In Troy, there lies the scene. From Isles of Greece
> The princes orgulous, their high blood chaf'd,   (=haughty)
> Have to the port of Athens sent their ships
> Fraught with the ministers and instruments
> Of cruel war: sixty and nine that wore
> Their crownets regal, from th'Athenian bay
> Put forth toward Phrygia, and their vow is made
> To ransack Troy, within whose strong immures   (walls)
> The ravish'd Helen, Menelaus' queen,
> With wanton Paris sleeps – and that's the quarrel.   (T&C Prol.)

But the quarrel ceases to motivate Troilus:

> (An alarum is heard)
> Peace, you ungracious clamours! peace, rude sounds!
> Fools on both sides! Helen must needs be fair,
> When with your blood you daily paint her thus.
> I cannot fight upon this argument:
> It is too starved a subject for my sword.   (1.1.89)

Caustic Thersites is even more forthright:

> Here is such patchery, such juggling, and such knavery!
> All the argument is a whore and a cuckold: a good quarrel
> To draw emulous factions, and bleed to death upon. Now the
> dry serpigo on the subject, and war and lechery confound all!
>
>   (2.3.78)
>   (serpigo= general term for skin disease)

Women have been trophies of war since long before the rape of the Sabine women by the warriors of ancient Rome. Rape was an accepted perquisite for victorious soldiers, as we see acknowledged in Henry the Fifth's threat to besieged Harfleur:

> How yet resolves the governor of the town?
> This is the latest parle we will admit:

Therefore to our best mercy give yourselves;
Or like to men proud of destruction
Defy us to our worst: for, as I am a soldier,
A name that in my thoughts becomes me best,
If I begin the batt'ry once again,
I will not leave the half-achiev'd Harfleur
Till in her ashes she lie buried.
The gates of mercy shall be all shut up,
And the flesh'd soldier, rough and hard of heart,
In liberty of bloody hand shall range
With conscience wide as hell, mowing like grass
Your fresh-fair virgins and your flow'ring infants...
... What is't to me, when you yourselves are cause,
If your pure maidens fall into the hand
Of hot and forcing violation?...
                                    ... look to see
The blind and bloody soldier with foul hand
Defile the locks of your shrill-shrieking daughters.   (3.3.1)

When the town surrendered it was placed under the supervision of
Sir John Fastolf, and one of his garrison was called Bardolf.

War is such a savage remedy that the ground and reason for it must
first be carefully weighed and seen to be justified. As he considers
whether to invade France, Henry calls upon the Archbishop of Canterbury and the Bishop of Ely for advice concerning his claim to the throne
of France:

... God forbid, my dear and faithful lord,
That you should fashion, wrest, or bow your reading, (interpretation)
Or nicely charge your understanding soul
With opening titles miscreate, whose right   (unlawful claims)
Suits not in native colours with the truth;
For God doth know how many now in health
Shall drop their blood in approbation
Of what your reverence shall incite us to.
Therefore take heed...
How you awake our sleeping sword of war:
We charge you, in the name of God, take heed;
For never two such kingdoms did contend
Without much fall of blood; whose guiltless drops
Are every one a woe, a sore complaint

'Gainst him whose wrongs gives edge unto the swords
That makes such waste in brief mortality.   (1.2.13)

The conversation between the disguised King Henry and his soldiers
on the eve of battle is one of the most brilliant examples of Shakespeare's
imagination. Typically, he gives each side credible arguments for and
against war:

(King Henry, disguised:) ... methinks I could not die anywhere
so contented as in the king's company, his cause being just and
his quarrel honourable.
(Michael Williams:) That's more than we know...
... if the cause be not good, the king himself hath a heavy reckoning to make; when all those legs and arms and heads, chopped
off in a battle, shall join together at the latter day, and cry all,"We
died at such a place"; some swearing, some crying for a surgeon,
some upon their wives left poor behind them, some upon the
debts they owe, some upon their children rawly left. I am afeard
there are few die well that die in a battle; for how can they chari-
tably dispose of any thing when blood is their argument? Now,
if these men do not die well, it will be a black matter for the king
that led them to it...   (4.1.128)

For the prelude to this scene, see p.108

Some wars may be undertaken to divert public attention from problems at home. The dying Henry IVth, fearing murmurings and sedition
in England, advises his son and successor:

Therefore, my Harry,
Be it thy course to busy giddy minds
With foreign quarrels   (2 Hy IV 4.5.212)

If wars must happen, then in general those on the side of justice, freedom and human rights tend to fight with more determination:

(King Henry VIth:)
What stronger breastplate than a heart untainted!
Thrice is he arm'd that hath his quarrel just,
And he but naked, though lock'd up in steel,
Whose conscience with injustice is corrupted.   (2 Hy VI 3.2.232)

Once war breaks out, rational judgement is suspended, and the spirit
of patriotism and excitement carries young men away to join the conflict.

82

Here is a line from All's Well that Ends Well:

> To the wars, my boy! to the wars!   (2.3.295)

In Coriolanus the talk is that war is imminent:

> (First Servant:) But when goes this forward?
>
> (Third Servant:) Tomorrow; today; presently; you shall have the drum struck up this afternoon. .
>
> (Second Servant:) Why, then we shall have a stirring world again. This peace is good for nothing but to rust iron, increase tailors, and breed ballad-makers.
>
> (1st Serv:) Let me have war, say I. It exceeds peace as far as day does night: it's sprightly, waking, audible, and full of vent. Peace is a very apoplexy, lethargy; mulled, deaf, sleepy, insensible; a getter of more bastard children than war's a destroyer of men.
>
> (2nd Serv:) 'Tis so, and as wars, in some sort, may be said to be a ravisher, so it cannot be denied but peace is a great maker of cuckolds.
>
> (1st Serv:) Ay, and it makes men hate one another.
>
> (3rd Serv:) Reason: because they then less need one another. The wars for my money.   (4.5.229)

The Chorus in Henry Vth conveys the atmosphere prevailing at the outbreak of war;

> Now all the youth of England are on fire,
> And silken dalliance in the wardrobe lies:
> Now thrive the armourers, and honour's thought
> Reigns solely in the breast of every man.
> They sell the pasture now to buy the horse...
> ... For now sits Expectation in the air

What wonderful images are compressed into those few lines! Since Shakespeare's Henry Vth is the play most intimately involved with war, this chapter must continue to draw episodes from it. It is clear that, despite the King's riotous youth, his character has been elevated to that of the ideal monarch*. Early in the play the Archbishop of Canterbury refers to him as a scholar, and goes on:

> Hear him but reason in divinity,
> And, all-admiring, with an inward wish

---

*   see further consideration of this in the chapter on The State.

You would desire the king were made a prelate:
Here him debate of commonwealth affairs,
You would say it hath been all in all his study:
List his discourse of war, and you shall hear
A fearful battle render'd you in music:
Turn him to any cause of policy,
The Gordian knot of it he will unloose...   (1.1.38)

The Chorus to Act 2 calls Henry "the mirror of all Christian kings."
At the siege of Harfleur we get the first of Henry's great rallying cries to
his troops, hackneyed in repetition perhaps, but he would be a stone to
remain unmoved by the soaring spirit of it:

Once more unto the breach, dear friends, once more,
Or close the wall up with our English dead.
In peace there's nothing so becomes a man
As modest stillness and humility:
But when the blast of war blows in our ears,
Then imitate the action of the tiger;
Stiffen the sinews, conjure up the blood,
Disguise fair nature with hard -favour'd rage...
... Now set the teeth and stretch the nostril wide,
Hold hard the breath, and bend up every spirit
To his full height! On, on, you noblest English! ...
...   And you, good yeomen,
Whose limbs were made in England, show us here
The mettle of your pasture; let us swear
That you are worth your breeding; which I doubt not;
For there is none of you so mean and base
That hath not noble lustre in your eyes.
I see you stand like greyhounds in the slips,
Straining upon the start. The game's afoot:
Follow your spirit; and upon this charge
Cry, "God for Harry, England, and Saint George!"   (3.1.1)

A note should be added here: the more familiar '*summon* up the
blood' dates only from Nicholas Rowe's interpretation (1709) of an am-
biguous spelling in the original Folio.

But in case the description of the warriors as 'you noblest English'
should strain credulity too far, Shakespeare brings us back to earth with
his portrayal of the rascality of the common soldiers. They, after all, are

the same men that Henry has warned are capable of committing rape, murder and pillage among the civilian population of Harfleur.

In Henry IV, Part 2, we have made the acquaintance of Ancient Pistol, 'a swaggering rascal', 'foul-mouthed rogue' and 'cut-purse'. The word 'Ancient' signifies a standard-bearer. His characteristic manner of speech is a bombastic, mock-poetic style:

> (Pistol:) Bardolph, a soldier firm and sound of heart,
> And of buxom valour, hath, by cruel fate
> And giddy Fortune's furious fickle wheel,
> That goddess blind,
> That stands upon the rolling restless stone…
> … Fortune is Bardolph's foe, and frowns on him;
> For he hath stol'n a pax, and hanged must a' be.
> A damnèd death!
> Let gallows gape for dog, let man go free,
> And let not hemp his wind-pipe suffocate.
> But Exeter hath given the doom of death   (Duke of Exeter)
> For pax of little price.   (Hy V 3.6.26)

He means a pyx, a sacred vessel containing the sacrament. Gower, an English captain, has the measure of Pistol:

Why, this is an arrant counterfeit rascal: I remember him now; a bawd, a cut-purse…

… Why, 'tis a gull, a fool, a rogue, that now and then goes to the wars to grace himself at his return into London under the form of a soldier. And such fellows are perfect in the great commanders' names, and they will learn you by rote where services were done; at such and such a sconce (fort), at such a breach, at such a convoy; who came off bravely, who was shot, who disgraced, what terms the enemy stood on; and this they con perfectly in the phrase of war, which they trick up with new-tuned oaths: and what a beard of the general's cut and a horrid suit of the camp will do among foaming bottles and ale-washed wits, is wonderful to be thought on.   (3.6.63)

Shakespeare creates the figure of Captain Fluellen, a kindly caricature of an honest Welshman. The name is an Englishman's attempt to get his tongue around 'Llywelyn'. The king arrives on the scene, to see how the action is progressing:

> (K.Hen:) How now, Fluellen! cam'st thou from the bridge?
> (Flu:) Ay, so please your majesty. The Duke of Exeter has very

gallantly maintained the pridge: the French is gone off, look you...

(K.Hen:) What men have you lost, Fluellen?

(Flu:) The perdition of th'athversary hath been very great, reasonable great: marry, for my part, I think the duke hath lost never a man but one that is like to be executed for robbing a church; one Bardolph, if your majesty know the man: his face is all bubuckles, and whelks, and knobs, and flames o'fire; and his lips blows at his nose, and it is like a coal of fire, sometimes plue and sometimes red; but his nose is executed, and his fire's out.

(K.Hen:) We would have all such offenders so cut off: and we give express charge that in our marches through the country there be nothing compelled from the villages, nothing taken but paid for, none of the French upbraided or abused in disdainful language; for when lenity and cruelty play for a kingdom, the gentlest gamester is the soonest winner.   (3.6.92)

Those are noble sentiments indeed, but probably Shakespeare's rather than Henry's, for it is known that he was implacable in refusing succour to civilians at the siege of Rouen and elsewhere, and when his soldiers wanted to share their bread with such wretches, he forbade it. Holinshed records that Henry had previously given orders forbidding theft from churches:

> yf Any... of our hooste presume to take Awaye frome Any churche... Any of theyr goodes, that ys, to saye vestments, chalices, books, Iuwells, or Any Relyques ... they be forthwith hanged therefore... no man vnder payne of dethe be so bolde As to touche onreuerently the sacrament of the Auter, or the pyxe, or Any other boxe wherein yt ys conteyned.

Bardolph's theft is based on Holinshed:

> A souldier (took) a pix out of a church, for which he was apprehended, & the king not once removed till the box was restored, and the offender strangled.

The climax of the play is of course the battle of Agincourt. Henry's army, weakened by fatigue and sickness, were struggling to reach Calais and England, but had their way barred by a French army at least four times as numerous. Henry according to Holinshed, "calling his captains and soldiers about him, he made to them a right grave oration, moving them to play the men, whereby to obtain a glorious victory... To conclude, many words of courage he uttered, to stir them to do manfully...

It is said that as he heard one of the host utter his wish to another thus: 'I would to God there were with us now so many good soldiers as are at this hour within England!' the King answered: 'I would not wish a man more here than I have; we are indeed in comparison to the enemies but a few, but if God of his clemency do favour us and our just cause (as I trust he will) we shall speed well enough... '"

Using the hints contained in Holinshed's straightforward prose, Shakespeare constructs out of his imagination speeches of imperishable poetry and power. When I say imagination, I mean he actually imagines he is at that scene, and in the mind of the king. For that reason, what we hear is convincingly the language we would expect from a medieval king and a leader of men, in that moment of danger.

> (The Earl of Westmoreland:) O that we now had here
> But one ten thousand of those men in England
> That do no work today!　　　　(a 'holy-day' in honour of St.Crispian)
> (K.Hen:)　　　　　　What's he that wishes so?
> My cousin Westmoreland? No, my fair cousin:
> If we are mark'd to die, we are enow
> To do our country loss; and if we live,
> The fewer men, the greater share of honour.
> God's will! I pray thee, wish not one man more.
> By Jove, I am not covetous for gold,
> Nor care I who doth feed upon my cost;
> It earns me not if men my garments wear;　　　(earns=grieves)
> Such outward things dwell not in my desires:
> But if it be a sin to covet honour,
> I am the most offending soul alive.
> No, faith, my coz, wish not a man from England:
> God's peace! I would not lose so great an honour
> As one man more, methinks, would share from me,
> For the best hope I have. O, do not wish one more!
> Rather proclaim it, Westmoreland, through my host,
> That he which hath no stomach to this fight,
> Let him depart; his passport shall be made,
> And crowns for convoy put into his purse:
> We would not die in that man's company
> That fears his fellowship to die with us.
> This day is call'd the feast of Crispian:

He that outlives this day, and comes safe home,
Will stand a-tiptoe when this day is nam'd,
And rouse him at the name of Crispian.
He that shall see this day, and live old age,
Will yearly on the vigil feast his neighbours,
And say," Tomorrow is Saint Crispian";
Then will he strip his sleeve and show his scars,
And say, "These wounds I had on Crispin's day".
Old men forget; yet all shall be forgot,   (line in Q, not F)
But he'll remember, with advantages,
What feats he did that day. Then shall our names,
Familiar in his mouth as household words,
Harry the King, Bedford and Exeter,
Warwick and Talbot, Salisbury and Gloucester,
Be in their flowing cups freshly rememb'rèd.
This story shall the good man teach his son;
And Crispin Crispian shall ne'er go by,
From this day to the ending of the world,
But we in it shall be rememberèd;
We few, we happy few, we band of brothers;
For he today that sheds his blood with me
Shall be my brother; be he ne'er so vile   (of lowly birth)
This day shall gentle his condition:
And gentlemen in England, now a-bed
Shall I think themselves accurs'd they were not here,
And hold their manhoods cheap whiles any speaks
That fought with us upon Saint Crispin's day.   (4.3.16)

The feast of St Crispian was celebrated on October 25th. The brothers Crispinus and Crispianus, patron saints of shoemakers, fled from Rome to Soissons (Roman Suessiona) during the Diocletian persecution. They introduced Christianity to Soissons, and worked there as shoemakers, but suffered martyrdom in 297. "Jove" was probably "God" in the original play, but altered to avoid contravening an Act of 1605 forbidding profanity on the stage. 'Gentle his condition' implies 'make him a gentleman'. It is interesting to find that in 1418 the king gave orders to the Sheriff of Southampton limiting the issue of coats of arms, making an exception for 'those who bare arms with us at the battle of Agincourt'. When the victory is won, Henry ascribes it to divine intervention:

'O God, thy arm was here;
And not to us, but to thy arm alone,
                    ascribe we all!'

After Shakespeare has carried us into the pit of 'all-abhorrèd war', he returns us to the thoughts of peace, embodied in the Duke of Burgundy's solemn and moving appeal to the two kings:

Great Kings of France and England! That I have labour'd
With all my wits, my pains, and strong endeavours,
To bring your most imperial majesties
Unto this bar and royal interview,   (like a bar of justice)
Your mightiness on both parts best can witness.
Since then my office hath so far prevail'd
That face to face, and royal eye to eye,
You have congreeted, let it not disgrace me
If I demand before this royal view,
What rub or what impediment there is,
Why that the naked, poor, and mangled Peace,
Dear nurse of arts, plenties, and joyful births,
Should not in this best garden of the world,
Our fertile France, put up her lovely visage?
Alas! She hath from France too long been chas'd
And all her husbandry doth lie on heaps,
Corrupting in its own fertility.   (*it* in F)(5.2.24)

The rest of this passage has already been quoted in the earlier chapter dealing with the natural world, for it lists a wonderful range of the weeds that have smothered the neglected vineyards and meadows, once more demonstrating Shakespeare's close observation of the countryside and his attachment to it.

At the end of Henry Vth, Shakespeare provides us with a nice contrast between the triumphant homecoming of the King, and the less-honoured homecoming of Pistol, the typical amoral common soldier who, when peace comes, has to learn to survive by fair means or foul. First, the audience is asked to imagine "upon your wingèd thoughts" the King's return after Agincourt:

(Chorus, Act 5)

        Behold the English beach
Pales in the flood with men, with wives, and boys,
Whose shouts and claps out-voice the deep -mouth'd sea,

Which, like a mighty whiffler, 'fore the king   (official, clearing-way
Seems to prepare his way: so let him land,   for procession)
And solemnly see him set on to London.
So swift a pace hath thought that even now
You may imagine him upon Blackheath;
Where that his lords desire him to have borne
His bruisèd helmet and his bended sword   (his Agincourt helmet is
Before him through the city: he forbids it,   preserved in Westminster
Being free from vainness and self- glorious pride;   Abbey)
Giving full trophy, signal and ostent,
Quite from himself, to God. But now behold,
In the quick forge and working-house of thought,
How London doth pour out her citizens!
The mayor and all his brethren in best sort,   (array)
Like to the senators of th'antique Rome,
With the plebeians swarming at their heels,
Go forth and fetch their conqu'ring Caesar in...   (Chorus, Act 5)

Pistol had been frank about his intentions from the start:
Let us to France, like horse-leeches, my boys,
To suck, to suck, the very blood to suck!   (2.4.56)
Now Fortune's wheel keeps turning:
(Pistol:) Doth Fortune play the huswife with me now?   (hussy)
News have I that my Doll is dead i' th' spital   (hospital)
Of malady of France;   (V.D.)
And there my rendezvous is quite cut off.
Old do I wax, and from my weary limbs
Honour is cudgell'd. Well, bawd I'll turn,
And something lean to cut-purse of quick hand.
To England will I steal, and there I'll steal:
And patches will I get unto these cudgell'd scars,
And swear I got them in the Gallia wars.   (5.1.83)

Either Shakespeare or his editor slipped up here, for at the opening
of the play we are told that Pistol is married to Nell Quickly, and he
tells Nym to go to the hospital and 'espouse' Doll Tearsheet. The printer
might easily have interpreted badly written 'Nell' for 'Doll'.

In Henry IVth, Part 1, we are given another glimpse of the character
of common soldiers, as Falstaff leads his troop towards Shrewsbury and
the expected battle:

90

If I be not ashamed of my soldiers, I am a soused gurnet; I have misused the King's press damnably. I have got in exchange of a hundred and fifty soldiers three hundred and odd pounds. I press me none but good householders, yeomen's sons, inquire me out contracted bachelors, such as had been asked twice on the banns, such a commodity of warm slaves as had as lief hear the devil as a drum, such as fear the report of a caliver (musket) worse than a struck fowl or a hurt wild duck. I pressed me none but such toasts-and-butter, with hearts in their bellies no bigger than pins' heads, and they have bought out their services; and now my whole charge consists of ancients, corporals, lieutenants, gentlemen of companies – slaves as ragged as Lazarus in the painted cloth, where the glutton's dogs licked his sores: and such as indeed were never soldiers, but discarded unjust serving-men, younger sons to younger brothers, revolted tapsters, and ostlers trade-fallen, the cankers of a calm world and a long peace, ten times more dishonourable-ragged than an old fazed ancient; and such have I to fill up the rooms of them as have bought out their services, that you would think that I had a hundred and fifty tattered prodigals lately come from swine-keeping, from eating draff and husks. A mad fellow met me on the way, and told me I had unloaded all the gibbets and pressed the dead bodies. No eye hath seen such scarecrows. I'll not march through Coventry with them, that's flat: nay, and the villains march wide between the legs as if they had gyves on, for indeed I had the most of them out of prison. There's not a shirt and a half in all my company, and the half shirt is two napkins tacked together and thrown over the soldiers like a herald's coat without sleeves; and the shirt to say the truth stolen from my host at Saint Albans, or the red-nose inn-keeper of Daventry. But that's all one, they'll find linen enough on every hedge. (4.2.12)

Is there anywhere in the plays a more sustained torrent of invention and comic images? Performed on the stage, and delivered by a seasoned actor, this speech delights the audience. How much more the Elizabethan audience would have laughed, for every day they saw such scarecrows walking the streets. This passage requires a note or two. Pressing men into service, but then letting them off in return for a bribe must have been a common practice, judging by some lines in The Voyage to Cadiz, published in 1597:

a certaine Lieutenant was degraded and cashiered, &c.,
for the taking of money by the way of corruption of certain prest
souldiers in the country, and for placing of others in their rooms,
more unfit for service and of less sufficiency and abilitie.

In Henry IVth, Part 2, we witness Falstaff's scam in progress:
(Falstaff:) Fie! This is hot weather, gentlemen. Have you pro-
vided me here half a dozen sufficient men?
(Justice Shallow:) Marry, have we, sir. Will you sit?
(Falstaff:) Let me see them, I beseech you.
(Shallow:) Where's the roll? Where's the roll? Where's the roll?
Let me see, let me see, let me see. So, so, so, so, so, so, - so.
(3.2.102)

Then follows a hilarious selection process, of which we only have
space for one example:
(Falstaff:)   ... Who is next?
(Shallow:) Peter Bullcalf o' th' Green!
(Falstaff:) Yea, marry, let's see Bullcalf.
(Bullcalf:) Here, sir.
(Falstaff:) 'Fore God, a likely fellow! Come, prick Bullcalf till he
roar again.   (double meaning: mark on list, & goad)
(Bullcalf:) O Lord! good my lord captain –
(Falstaff:)   What! dost thou roar before thou art pricked?
(Bullcalf:)   O Lord, sir, I am a diseased man.
(Falstaff:)   What disease hast thou?
(Bullcalf:) A whoreson cold, sir, a cough, sir, which I caught with
ringing in the King's affairs upon his coronation day. sir.
(Falstaff:) Come, thou shalt go to the wars in a gown. We will
have away thy cold, and I will take such order that thy friends
shall ring for thee.   (3.2.184)

When Falstaff and the justices leave for dinner, Bullcalf does a deal
with Bardolph:
(Bullcalf:) Good Master Corporate Bardolph, stand my friend,
and here's four Harry ten shillings in French crowns for you. In
very truth, sir, I had as lief be hanged, sir, as go. And yet for mine
own part, sir, I do not care, but rather, because I am unwilling,
and, for mine own part, have a desire to stay with my friends.
Else, sir, I did not care, for mine own part, so much.

92

(Bardolph:) Go to, stand aside.

(Mouldy:) And, good Master Corporal Captain, for my dame's sake, stand my friend. She has nobody to do anything about her when I am gone, and she is old, and cannot help herself. You shall have forty, sir.   (forty shillings)

(Bardolph:) Go to, stand aside.   (3.2.238)

How true to life is the blethering from Bullcalf, uncomfortable with what he knows is shabby cowardice. Feeble is no such wimp:

(Feeble:) By my troth, I care not. A man can die but once. We owe God a death. I'll ne'er bear a base mind: an't be my destiny, so. An't be not, so. No man's too good to serve's Prince. And let it go which way it will, he that dies this year is quit for the next.

(Bardolph:) Well said. Thou'rt a good fellow.

(Feeble:) Faith, I'll bear no base mind.   (3.2.253)

When Falstaff returns, Bardolph has a private word with him:

(Bardolph:) Sir, a word with you. (Aside:) I have three pound to free Mouldy and Bullcalf.

(Falstaff:) Go to; well

(Shallow:) Come, Sir John, which four will you have?

(Falstaff:) Do you choose for me?

(Shallow:) Marry, then, Mouldy, Bullcalf, Feeble, and Shadow.

(Fal:) Mouldy and Bullcalf: for you, Mouldy, stay at home till you are past service. And for your part, Bullcalf, grow till you come unto it. I will none of you.

(Shallow:) Sir John, Sir John, do not yourself wrong: they are your likeliest men, and I would have you served with the best.

(Fal:) Will you tell me, Master Shallow, how to choose a man? Care I for the limb, the thews, the stature, bulk, and big assemblance of a man? Give me the spirit, Master Shallow! Here's Wart: you see what a ragged appearance it is. 'A shall charge you and discharge you with the motion of a pewterer's hammer, come off and on swifter than he that gibbets on the brewer's bucket. (i.e. hoists on brewer's crane) And this same half-faced fellow, Shadow, give me this man: he presents no mark to the enemy; the foeman may with as great aim level at the edge of a penknife. And, for a retreat, how swiftly will this Feeble the woman's tailor run off! O! give me the spare men, and spare me the great ones. Put me a caliver (musket) into Wart's hand, Bardolph.

93

(Bard:) Hold, Wart, traverse. Thus, thus, thus.   (traverse=thrust)
(Fal:) Come, manage me your caliver. So. Very well. Go to.
Very good, exceeding good. O, give me always a little, lean, old,
chopped, bald shot. Well said, I'faith, Wart. Thou'rt a good scab.
(=wart) Hold, there's a tester for thee.(sixpence)

Falstaff's cynicism concerning the quality of his soldiers is demonstrated in Henry IVth, Part 1:
(Prince Hal:) … tell me, Jack, whose fellows are these that come
after?
(Fal:) Mine, Hal, mine.
(Prince:) I did never see such pitiful rascals
(Fal:) Tut, tut, good enough to toss, food for powder, food for
powder, they'll fill a pit as well as better; tush, man, mortal men,
mortal men.   (4.2.68)

In a later war, such men became, in that dreadful phrase, 'cannon fod-
der.' In Shakespeare's time, if captains lost their men, they could pocket
the unclaimed wages.

This chapter promised a reference to patriotism. It is useless to look
for that word in Shakespeare, for it was only introduced to the language
in 1726. However, it was his friend Ben Jonson who first gave a name
to the concept: 'Such as were known as patriots, sound lovers of their
country.' That was in 1596. Love of country can be simply an emotional
attachment to the place where you were brought up, the place where you
feel comfortable with like-minded folk, in short the place that is home.
When that homeland is threatened, as during the reign of Elizabeth, the
emotion strengthens and becomes a determination to defend it against
those who would destroy it. Here are the final lines of King John:
This England never did, nor never shall,
Lie at the proud foot of a conqueror,
But when it first did help to wound itself…
… Come the three corners of the world in arms,
And we shall shock them. Nought shall make us rue,
If England to itself do rest but true.   (5.7.112)

If we talk of patriotism, the reader will guess that sooner or later we
must come to the great speech of John of Gaunt in Richard IInd. The
content of the speech seems to be entirely the creation of Shakespeare's
imagination, and owes little or nothing to the actual character of the his-

torical Duke of Lancaster, who appears to have been grasping, lacking in wisdom and an adulterer, and who was both the most powerful and at the same time the most unpopular man in England. The speech, therefore, is Shakespeare's own celebration of the spirit of his homeland, expressed in language that rises to the highest level of poetry. It is not a great call to arms, nor a denigration of other nations, who are presumably entitled to their own hymns of praise. Those who quote only the patriotic bits forget that the speech has a sting in the tail, comparing the ideal of what might be with the reality of what is, namely a decay of old values and a woeful failure of royal government. Shakespeare probably took some lines out of Lord Berners' translation of Froissart as his starting point:

> So it fell that about the feast of Christmas, Duke John of Lancaster, who lived in great displeasure, what because the king had banished his son out of the realm for so little a cause, and also because of the evil governing of the realm by his nephew King Richard: for he saw well that if he long persevered and were suffered to continue, the realm was likely to be utterly lost; with these imaginations and other, the Duke fell sick, whereon he died, whose death was greatly sorrowed of all his friends and lovers, The King, by what he showed, took no great care for his death, but soon he was forgotten.

The scene is set as sick Gaunt talks to his brother, the Duke of York, about the king's inadequacies and mismanagement:

> (Gaunt:) Will the king come that I may breathe my last
> In wholesome counsel to his unstaid youth?
> (York:) Vex not yourself, nor strive not with your breath;
> For all in vain comes counsel to his ear.
> (Gaunt:) O, but they say the tongues of dying men
> Inforce attention like deep harmony.
> Where words are scarce they are seldom spent in vain,
> For they breathe truth that breathe their words in pain.
> He that no more must say is listened more
> Than they whom youth and ease have taught to glose;   (flatter)
> More are men's ends marked than their lives before.
> The setting sun, and music at the close,
> As the last taste of sweets, is sweetest last,
> Writ in remembrance more than things long past:
> Though Richard my life's counsel would not hear,
> My death's sad tale may yet undeaf his ear.

(York:) No, it is stopped with other flattering sounds
As praises, of whose taste the wise are fond,
Lascivious metres, to whose venom sound
The open ear of youth doth always listen,
Report of fashions in proud Italy,
Whose manners still our tardy-apish nation   (slow to copy)
Limps after in base imitation.
Where doth the world thrust forth a vanity –
So it be new, there's no respect how vile –
That is not quickly buzzed into his ears?
Then all too late comes counsel to be heard,
Where will doth mutiny with wit's regard.   (will vs. reason)
Direct not him whose way himself will choose:
'Tis breath thou lack'st, and that breath wilt thou lose.
(Gaunt:) Methinks I am a prophet new-inspir'd,
And thus expiring do foretell of him:
His rash fierce blaze of riot cannot last,
For violent fires soon burn out themselves;
Small showers last long, but sudden storms are short;
He tires betimes that spurs too fast betimes;
With eager feeding food doth choke the feeder;
Light vanity, insatiate cormorant,   (bird supposedly gluttonous)
Consuming means, soon preys upon itself.
This royal throne of kings, this sceptred isle,
This earth of majesty, this seat of Mars,
This other Eden, demi-paradise,
This fortress built by Nature for herself
Against infection and the hand of war,
This happy breed of men, this little world,
This precious stone set in the silver sea,
Which serves it in the office of a wall,
Or as a moat defensive to a house,
Against the envy of less happier lands;
This blessed plot, this earth, this realm, this England,
This nurse, this teeming womb of royal kings,
Feared by their breed, and famous by their birth,
Renownèd for their deeds as far from home,
For Christian service and true chivalry,
As is the sepulchre in stubborn Jewry
Of the world's ransom, blessed Mary's son;

This land of such dear souls, this dear, dear land,
Dear for her reputation through the world,
Is now leased out – I die pronouncing it –
Like to a tenement or pelting farm. (petty,paltry)
England, bound in with the triumphant sea,
Whose rocky shore beats back the envious siege
Of watery Neptune, is now bound in with shame,
With inky blots and rotten parchment bonds;
That England, that was wont to conquer others,
Hath made a shameful conquest of itself.
Ah, would the scandal vanish with my life,
How happy then were my ensuing death! (Rd II 2.1.1)

To add notes seems an insult to the clarity of thought and noble language displayed here. Nevertheless, some comments may be found helpful. A typical Shakespeare touch is the repetition of words, such as 'this' hammered at us, and holding everything together. 'Dear' is another word which gains by repetition. The concept of the land as a jewel in the silver mounting of the sea is a brilliant metaphor, and the repeated sibilants echo the sound of the sea itself, as do the onomatopoeic 'triumphant sea' and 'envious siege' later on.

THE STATE: ORDER & AUTHORITY.

Before we consider Shakespeare's views on politics it is important to point out that we should not expect to find any deep social or historical analysis in the plays, such as one gets for example in a play by Bernard Shaw. They were written to entertain during 'the two hours traffic of our stage', developing the universal themes calculated to hold the attention of the audience – love, comedy, war, treachery, death. Our author was more interested in the creation of credible portraits of individuals and imagining how they might react to here-and-now moral dilemmas. Any more profound philosophising would have bored the spectators and killed the entertainment stone dead.

Shakespeare has been hailed as the universal man, with something significant to say about human character which has been found relevant for all individuals in all countries and in all ages up to our own. But when we come to study his views on politics, we will have to revise that opinion, and recognise he was a child of his time, and that his outlook is not necessarily ours. Human nature may not have changed, but (at least in the West) political structures have altered out of all recognition. Since his time there have been revolutions in thought and politics, and in more than one country monarchs have been executed by their subjects.

As he grew up, he would have accepted the prevailing philosophy underpinning the structure of the state. This philosophy is summed up in the Homily of Obedience, contained in the Book of Homilies, pub-lished in 1547, one of a series of sermons intended to be read in church. Here is an excerpt:

> Almighty God hath created and appointed all things, in heaven, earth and waters, in a most excellent and perfect order. In heaven he hath appointed distinct orders and states of archan-gels and angels. In the earth he hath assigned kings, princes, with other governors under them, all in good and necessary order.

The author goes on to assert that the same order is to be found in the behaviour of the heavenly bodies, the seasons and in the whole of nature.

98

And man himself also hath all his parts, both within and without, as soul, heart, mind, memory, understanding, reason, speech, with all and singular corporal members of his body, in a profitable, necessary and pleasant order. Every degree of people, in their vocation, calling, and office, hath appointed to them their duty and order. Some are in high degree, some in low, some kings and princes, some inferiors and subjects, priests and laymen, masters and servants, fathers and children, husbands and wives, rich and poor, and every one hath need of other, so that in all things is to be praised the goodly order of God, without the which, no house, no city, no commonwealth, can continue and endure. For where there is no right order, there reigneth all abuse, carnal liberty, enormity, sin, and Babylonical confusion. Take away kings, princes, rulers, magistrates, judges, and such states of God's order, no man shall ride or go by the highway unrobbed, no man shall sleep in his own house or bed unkilled, no man shall keep his wife, children and possessions in quietness, all things shall be common, and there must needs follow all mischief and utter destruction, both of souls, bodies, goods and commonwealths.

Some writers of that age followed St. Paul in comparing the body politic to an actual human body, where every organ has its part to play in maintaining an ordered whole. One such writer was Nicholas Breton, in a pamphlet called A Murmurer, being an attack on murmurers who want to undermine the government and the existing hierarchies of power. This extract shows his train of thought:

God made all the parts of the body for the soul and with the soul to serve him, and all the subjects in a kingdom to serve their king and with their king to serve him. If the head of the body ache, will not the heart be greatly grieved, and every part feel his part of the pain of it? ... No more can the council, the eye of the commonwealth, be disturbed, but the king will find it and the commonwealth will feel it... Can the labourer, the foot, be wounded, but the body of the state will feel it... ? And can the commonwealth, the body, be diseased, but the king, his council and every true subject will put to his hand for the help of it?

Similar ideas were expressed by Thomas Starkey, chaplain to King Henry VIII, in a work entitled Dialogue between Cardinal Pole and

Thomas Lupset:

> Like as in every man there is a body and also a soul in whose flourishing and prosperous state both together standeth the weal and felicity of man; so likewise there is in every commonalty city and country as it were a politic body and another thing also resembling the soul of man, in whose flourishing both together resteth also the true common weal. This body is nothing else but the multitude of people, the number of citizens in every commonalty city or country. The thing which is resembled to the soul is civil order and politic law, administered by officers and rulers. ... so doth the multitude of people in every country receive, as it were, civil life by laws well administered by good officers and wise rulers, by whom they be governed and kept in politic order.

Of course, from a modern prospective, we can see that the body analogy will not bear close examination, and in any case we have to ask the question: what happens if the last sentence should happen to read 'badly administered by corrupt officers and despotic rulers'? This political philosophy is poles apart from Abraham Lincoln's 'government of the people by the people for the people', and 'no man is good enough to govern another without that other's consent.' But it is easy to be judgmental with hindsight. To return to the point, which is that the foregoing passages sum up the prevailing political outlook of Shakespeare's age, so we must not complain if his writing reflects that.

In Troilus and Cressida, the Greek army has been besieging Troy for seven years without success, and King Agamemnon and his generals discuss why they have so far failed. Ulysses suggests that envy of rank has eaten away at the natural hierarchy which should exist in an army:

> The heavens themselves, the planets, and this centre   (the Earth)
> Observe degree, priority, and place,
> Insisture, course, proportion, season, form,   (I=steady motion)
> Office, and custom, in all line of order...
>   ... O, when degree is shaked,
> Which is the ladder of all high designs,
> The enterprise is sick. How could communities,
> Degrees in schools, and brotherhoods in cities,
> Peaceful commerce from dividable shore,   (=separated?)
>   The primogenity and due of birth,
> Prerogative of age, crowns, sceptres,laurels,

But by degree stand in authentic place?
Take but degree away, untune that string,
And hark what discord follows. Each thing melts   (melts in Q
In mere oppugnancy; the bounded waters   meets in F)
Should lift their bosoms higher than the shores,
And make a sop of all this solid globe;
Strength should be lord of imbecility,
And the rude son should strike his father dead;
Force should be right – or rather, right and wrong,
Between whose endless jar justice resides,
Should lose their names, and so should justice too.
Then everything includes itself in power,
Power into will, will into appetite,
And appetite, an universal wolf,
So doubly seconded with will and power,
Must make perforce an universal prey,
And last eat up itself.   (1.3.85)

We may not share Shakespeare's belief in such a hierarchy, a kind of pyramid with a monarch at the apex, supported by generals, governors and justices in the upper ranks, merchants, craftsmen and farmers forming the solid centre, all resting on a base composed of serfs and peasants, 'the mutable rank-scented many'. In such a caste system each individual must rest content with the rank assigned to him by divine decree.

Nevertheless, everyone would agree that order is better than anarchy, and Shakespeare obviously had a fear of the latter, a fear which was probably justified in view of the unstable history of that age. We must remember too that he had written a whole cycle of plays based on the struggle for the throne, the supreme power in the state, during the Wars of the Roses. By comparison with those earlier reigns, that of Elizabeth was a golden age of stability and prosperity. In the play King Henry VIII, the birth of Elizabeth is hailed by Archbishop Cranmer in Shakespeare's words:

This royal infant, - heaven still move about her! –
Though in her cradle, yet now promises
Upon this land a thousand thousand blessings,
Which time shall bring to ripeness: she shall be –
But few now living can behold that goodness –
A pattern to all princes living with her,
And all that shall succeed…   (5.5.18)

And after more praise in the same vein the speech continues:

> She shall be loved and feared; her own shall bless her;
> Her foes shake like a field of beaten corn,
> And hang their heads with sorrow; good grows with her.
> In her days every man shall eat in safety
> Under his own vine what he plants; and sing
> The merry songs of peace to all his neighbours.
> God shall be truly known; and those about her
> From her shall read the perfect ways of honour,
> And by those claim their greatness, not by blood.

That last sentence seems to contradict the fixed hierarchy of inherited degree laid down in Ulysses' speech. In fact Shakespeare's age was one of social mobility The price of land was falling (the market glutted after the sell-off of monastic estates), and that hit the land-owning class, but benefited the tenant farmers, some of whom bought land and moved up the scale. Other groups on the rise included lawyers and merchants, who often bought themselves country estates. During Tudor times several high officers of state came from humble backgrounds, including figures who appear in Shakespeare's Henry VIII: Wolsey's father was a butcher, Thomas Cromwell's was a blacksmith and brewer. Bishop Latimer and William Cecil, Elizabeth's principal adviser, came from yeoman stock.

Shakespeare himself was conscious of the need to better his social standing, and in 1596, in the name of his father John, he applied for the right to bear a coat of arms, and no fewer than five of his fellow actors did the same. In Henry IV, Part 2, Falstaff ridicules the social climbing of Justice Shallow:

> I do see the bottom of Justice Shallow. Lord, Lord! how subject we old men are to this vice of lying. This same starved justice hath done nothing but prate to me of the wildness of his youth and the feats he hath done about Turnbull Street, and every third word a lie... And now is this Vice's dagger become a squire, and talks as familiarly of John a Gaunt as if he had been sworn brother to him; and I'll be sworn a' never saw him but once in the Tilt-yard ... and now he has land and beeves.
>
> (Turnbull Street=brothel area)(3.2.328)

The following satirical poem, even though written 30 years after Shakespeare's day, comments on this 'nouveaux riches' phenomenon:

> I now have liv'd to see the day,

Wherein a fig-man beares such sway,
    that knights dare scarce sit by him;
Yea, I have liv'd to see the houre,
In which a clothier hath such power,
    that lords are glad to buy him.
Thus doe the froth of all the earth,
A spawne sprung from a dunghill birth,
    now prince it in our land:
A people come the Lord knowes how,
Both fame and nameless till just now,
    Must everyone command.   (Willis: Time's Whirligig)

Shakespeare must have seen these changes, but they may have made him apprehensive that the ordered society he approved of might fall apart. But whatever his views about that, there can be no doubt that he believed in monarchy, providing a strong guiding hand at the summit of the whole edifice, and that belief seemed to be amply justified while the throne was occupied by Elizabeth, a ruler of exceptional ability and dedication. But in fact her position was far from secure. She had been declared illegitimate by her own father, and had spent time in the Tower of London. She had no heir, and that meant that when she died there might be civil war between the various claimants to the throne. Two of her cousins who had a claim on the throne paid with their lives (Lady Jane Grey and Mary Queen of Scots). In 1570 she was excommunicated by the pope, who urged her Catholic subjects to depose her. In 1588 the Spanish Armada might have succeeded in doing that, had not the weather intervened, which it fortunately did again, to disperse two further Armada fleets in 1596 and 1597. Finally in 1601, there was an attempted coup d'état led by her one-time favourite, the Earl of Essex. The 'armado' referred to in King John 3.4.1 was probably that of 1596.

When we look at that constant threat of violence and usurpation lurking in the background, we are able to understand why Shakespeare believed in order and strong government. There are several passages where he pictures the dangers that surround a monarch. In this scene, Henry the Fourth, mortally sick, lies asleep, with the crown alongside him, and his son, Prince Hal, keeps watch beside him:

Why doth the crown lie there upon his pillow,
Being so troublesome a bedfellow?
O polished perturbation! golden care!
That keep'st the ports of slumber open wide

To many a watchful night! – sleep with it now!
Yet not so sound and deeply sweet
As he whose brow with homely biggin bound (=nightcap)
Snores out the watch of night. (2 Hy IV 4.5.20)

When Prince Hal eventually ascends the throne as King Henry the Fifth, Shakespeare gives him a soliloquy on the cares that fall upon the shoulders of a king. The scene is the night before the battle of Agincourt:

Upon the king! let us our lives, our souls,
Our debts, our careful wives,
Our children and our sins lay on the king!
We must bear all. O hard condition!
Twin-born with greatness, subject to the breath
Of every fool, whose sense no more can feel
But his own wringing. What infinite heart's ease (=stomach-ache)
Must kings neglect that private men enjoy!
And what have kings that privates have not too,
Save ceremony, save general ceremony?
And what art thou, thou idol ceremony?
What kind of god art thou, that suffer'st more
Of mortal griefs than do thy worshippers?
What are thy rents? what are thy comings-in?
O ceremony, show me but thy worth!
What is thy soul of adoration?
Art thou aught else but place, degree, and form,
Creating awe and fear in other men?
Wherein thou art less happy, being feared,
Than they in fearing.
What drink'st thou oft, instead of homage sweet,
But poisoned flattery? O be sick, great greatness,
And bid thy ceremony give thee cure!
Think'st thou the fiery fever will go out
With titles blown from adulation?
Will it give place to flexure and low-bending?
Canst thou, when thou command'st the beggars knee,
Command the health of it? No, thou proud dream,
That play'st so subtly with a king's repose;
I am a king that find thee; and I know
'Tis not the balm, the sceptre and the ball,

The sword, the mace, the crown imperial,
The intertissued robe of gold and pearl,
The farcèd title running 'fore the king,   (f=over-stuffed)
The throne he sits on, nor the tide of pomp
That beats upon the high shore of this world,
No, not all these, thrice-gorgeous ceremony,
Not all these, laid in bed majestical,
Can sleep so soundly as the wretched slave,
Who with a body filled and vacant mind
Gets him to rest, crammed with distressful bread;
Never sees horrid night, the child of hell,
But, like a lackey, from the rise to set
Sweats in the eye of Phoebus, and all night   (=the sun)
Sleeps in Elysium; next day after dawn,
Doth rise and help Hyperion to his horse,
And follows so the ever-running year
With profitable labour to his grave:
And, but for ceremony, such a wretch,
Winding up days with toil and nights with sleep,
Had the fore-hand and vantage of a king.
The slave, a member of the country's peace,
Enjoys it; but in gross little wots
What watch the king keeps to maintain the peace,
Whose hours the peasant best advantages.   (4.1.235)

This description of the burden carried by a monarch in earlier centuries would equally apply, in this more democratic age, to the awesome responsibility which rests on the shoulders of a prime minister or a president. But to Shakespeare, kings were more than elected heads of state, they were representatives of God himself, anointed by God's servants on earth, the bishops.

Not all the water in the rough rude sea
Can wash the balm from an anointed king;
The breath of worldly men cannot depose
The deputy elected by the Lord.   (Rd II 3.2.54)

That was Richard the Second, in defiant mood, before being deposed and supplanted by Henry Bolingbroke, who was duly anointed as King Henry the Fourth. Now his supporter Sir Walter Blount accuses the enemies of Henry: "You stand against anointed majesty." The Bishop of

Carlisle is a supporter of Richard as rightful king:

> What subject can give sentence on his king?

And the king is:

> the figure of God's majesty,
>   His captain, steward, deputy elect,
>   Anointed, crownèd, planted many years   (4.1.125)

The bishop continues:

>   My Lord of Hereford here, whom you call king,   (Bolingbroke)
>   Is a foul traitor to proud Hereford's king;
>   And if you crown him, let me prophesy,
>   The blood of English shall manure the ground
>   And future ages groan for this foul act;
>   Peace shall go sleep with Turks and infidels,
>   And in this seat of peace tumultuous wars
>   Shall kin with kin and kind with kind confound;
>   Disorder, horror, fear and mutiny
>   Shall here inhabit, and this land be called
>   The field of Golgotha and dead men's skulls.

That prophecy came true in the bloody wars of the Roses, the dynastic struggle for the throne between the supporters of the house of York (the white rose) and the supporters of the house of Lancaster (the red rose). No wonder Shakespeare feared a return to such strife, and was a profound believer in order and stability. Nevertheless, by an unlucky chance, he himself once came under suspicion of being associated with treason against the crown. One of Elizabeth's favourite courtiers was Robert Devereux, 2nd Earl of Essex, even though he was 33 years her junior. She gave him command of various expeditions against Spain, and made him earl marshal of England. In 1599 he was put in charge of a large force sent to Ireland to subdue a rebellion led by Hugh O'Neill, the great Earl of Tyrone. Elizabeth told Essex that for his expedition she gave him "power and authority more ample that ever any had, or ever shall have." He and his army left London with high hopes and the applause of the people thronging the streets. In Henry V, Shakespeare records the mood, and the expectation of a triumphant and victorious return to the capital:

>   Were now the general of our gracious empress –
>   As in good time he may – from Ireland coming,
>   Bringing rebellion broachèd on his sword,
>   How many would the peaceful city quit
>   To welcome him!   (Chorus, Act 5)

In Ireland Essex frittered away his resources on irrelevant and unsuccessful campaigns, and finally made peace in secret with Tyrone, who offered in return to help make Essex "the greatest man that ever was in England." That tempted Essex to return to London (against orders) with the intention of forcibly removing all the courtiers surrounding the Queen, making himself second only to her, and the main power in the land. Instead, he was scolded by Elizabeth, and held under house arrest. But his notorious vanity was wounded, and he gathered round himself "swordsmen, bold confident fellows, men of broken fortunes, discontented persons, and such as saucily used their tongues in railing against all men." In February 1601, he led this rag-tag army in a wild attempt to seize power, a total failure which led to his execution for high treason.

On the eve of the ill-fated rebellion the supporters of Essex persuaded the Chamberlain's Men, Shakespeare's company, to put on a special performance of his play Richard the Second, for the reason that it portrayed the deposition of a monarch, and at the trial of Essex it was alleged that he was "often present at the playing thereof ... with great applause giving countenance and liking to the same."

Strangely, the Chamberlain's Men acted the play before the Queen herself on the day before Essex went to the block, though for that performance the deposition scene was omitted. Another curious circumstance is related by the antiquary William Lambarde. He had drawn up a list of state documents and presented it to the Queen in August 1601. As she turned to documents of the reign of Richard IInd she said to Lambarde "I am Richard the Second, know ye not that?"

Henry Wriothesley, 3rd Earl of Southampton, was a patron and friend of Shakespeare. In 1599 it was said "My Lord Southampton and Lord Rutland come not to the court... They pass away the time in London merely in going to plays every day." Southampton was a close friend of the Earl of Essex, and accompanied him not only on two of his expeditions against the Spaniards, but also on his ill-fated Irish campaign. On his return from Ireland he was deeply involved with the attempted coup d'état, was put on trial and sentenced to death. Southampton had been ward of William Cecil, the great Lord Burghley, and his mother appealed to Robert Cecil, Burghley's son and secretary to the Queen "to pray mercy to my miserable son" with the result that the sentence of death was commuted to imprisonment in the Tower. Because of the special performance of Richard II, Augustine Phillips, representing Shakespeare and his fellow actors, was summoned before the Privy Council and closely questioned, but ultimately they were exonerated. In Shakespeare's case his close association with Southampton must have given him some anxious moments, but the dark cloud passed over.

Judging by parallels in the plays, Shakespeare must have been familiar with several books circulating in that age which defined the character of the ideal monarch. One such work was by Chelidonius, translated from Latin into French, and then again into English in 1571 under the title: Of the Institution and firste beginning of Christian Princes. Ideas from that book find many similarities in Henry the Fifth, notably the analogy of the beehive.

One characteristic of the ideal prince described in that book is that he should be familiar with the most humble of his subjects. King Richard the Second commented on the common touch shown by his rival, Henry Bolingbroke, and says that he had

> Observed his courtship to the common people,
> How he did seem to dive into their hearts
> With humble and familiar courtesy,
> What reverence he did throw away on slaves,
> Wooing poor craftsmen with the craft of smiles
> And patient underbearing of his fortune, (=acceptance of his banishment)
> ... Off goes his bonnet to an oyster-wench;
> A brace of draymen bid God speed him well,
> And had the tribute of his supple knee,
> With 'Thanks, my countrymen, my loving friends'   (1.4.24)

The most memorable example in Shakespeare of empathy between monarch and people is of course the "little touch of Harry in the night" when we see the king, Henry V, moving among and talking with his soldiers during the hours of darkness before the perilous battle yet to come:

> O, now, who will behold
> The royal captain of this ruined band
> Walking from watch to watch, from tent to tent,
> Let him cry, "Praise and glory on his head!"
> For forth he goes and visits all his host,
> Bids them good-morrow with a modest smile,
> And calls them brothers, friends and countrymen.
> Upon his royal face there is no note
> How dread an army hath enrounded him;
> Nor doth he dedicate one jot of colour   (i.e. his face shows no
> Unto the weary and all-watchèd night;   sign of sleeplessness)

But freshly looks and overbears attaint
With cheerful semblance and sweet majesty;
That every wretch, pining and pale before,
Beholding him, plucks comfort from his looks.
A largess universal like the sun
His liberal eye doth give to every one,
Thawing cold fear.   (Chorus, Act 4)

It is probable that Shakespeare had read an ancient account of the siege of Harfleur in which it was recorded that Henry "daylie and nightlie in his owne person visited and searched the watches, orders and stacions of everie part of his hoast, and whome he found diligent he praised and thanked, and the negligent he corrected and chastened." Perhaps taking his cue from that, he builds upon it with brilliant imagination, sending the king incognito from campfire to campfire:

(Williams:) Who goes there?

(K.Henry:) A friend.

(Williams:) Under what captain serve you?

(K.Henry:) Under Sir Thomas Erpingham.

(Williams:) A good old commander and a most kind gentleman: I pray you, what thinks he of our estate?

(K.Henry:) Even as men wracked upon a sand, that look to be washed off the next tide.

(Bates:) He hath not told his thought to the king?

(K.Henry:) No; nor is it not meet he should. For, though I speak it to you, I think the king is but a man, as I am: the violet smells to him as it doth to me; the element shows to him as it doth to me; all his senses have but human conditions: his ceremonies laid by, in his nakedness he appears but a man; and though his affections are higher mounted than ours, yet when they stoop, they stoop with the like wing. Therefore when he sees reason of fears, as we do, his fears, out of doubt, be of the same relish as ours are: yet, in reason, no man should possess him with any appearance of fear, lest he, by showing it, should dishearten his army.

(Bates:) He may show what outward courage he will, but I believe, as cold a night as 'tis, he could wish himself in Thames up to the neck, and so I would he were, and I by him, at all adventures, so we were quit here.

109

(K.Henry:) By my troth, I will speak my conscience of the king: I think he would not wish himself any where but where he is.

(4.1.91)

Incidentally, shortly after this passage, as Henry prays before the battle, he alludes to the illegitimacy of his father's seizure of the throne, and says what he has done in an attempt to atone for the wrong done to Richard:

Not today, O Lord!
O not today, think not upon the fault
My father made in compassing the crown!
I Richard's body have interrèd new,
And on it have bestowed more contrite tears
Than from it issued forcèd drops of blood.
Five hundred poor I have in yearly pay,
Who twice a day their withered hands hold up
Toward heaven, to pardon blood; and I have built
Two chantries, where the sad and solemn priests
Sing still for Richard's soul.   (4.1.297)

This passage closely follows Holinshed. After Richard banished Henry Bolingbroke, he treated the son with marked kindness and they became friends, so the respect expressed here is genuine.

In the same way that Shakespeare gives Henry V a speech in which he emphasizes the essential humanity and frailty of even the most exalted person in the state, so he puts a similar emotion into the mouth of Richard (note the effectiveness of monosyllables):

You have but mistook me all this while:
I live with bread like you, feel want,
Taste grief, need friends – subjected thus,
How can you say to me, I am a king?   (Rd II 3.2.174)

To return to the theme that the ideal monarch should be in touch with the most humble of his subjects: the reader may well ask, what have the qualities of medieval princes to do with the realities of life in the 21st Century? I would reply that we are looking at the ideal qualities suited to the chief servants of the state, whether they be presidents or prime ministers, and surely the ability to empathise with ordinary folk is a necessary quality in a leader. He or she must be able to understand the problems and environment of the most lowly citizen in the commonwealth, and haughty superiority is to be avoided like the plague.

110

A comment should be inserted here. Although Shakespeare lifted historical personages from the pages of Holinshed or Plutarch, he used his fertile imagination to mould them into whatever character suited the themes of his plays. In the case of the real Henry the Fifth, there is no doubt, according to the chroniclers, that he was a valiant warrior and an efficient administrator, but there is evidence that he had less than noble qualities in other areas. He was a religious bigot, and ordered the execution of hundreds of harmless Lollards, including his friend Sir John Oldcastle. He could be ruthless, notably seen in the butchery of the French prisoners after the battle of Agincourt. His glory-seeking French wars drained the wealth of England, devastated France (leaving a legacy of hatred), and were ultimately pointless, since all the conquests were soon lost. Shakespeare's early plays about Henry VI start with the funeral of Henry Vth:

> England ne'er had a king until his time,
> Virtue he had, deserving to command:
> His brandished sword did blind men with his beams;
> His arms spread wider than a dragon's wings;
> His sparkling eyes, replete with wrathful fire,
> More dazzled and drove back his enemies
> Than midday sun fierce bent against their faces.
> What should I say? His deeds exceed all speech:
> He ne'er lift up his hand but conquerèd.   (1 Hy VI 1.1.8)

But then a messenger arrives to spoil it all:

> Sad tidings bring I to you out of France,
> Of loss, of slaughter, and discomfiture:
> Guienne, Champaigne, Rheims, Orleans,
> Paris, Guysors, Poictiers, are all quite lost.

In some of the Roman plays Shakespeare portrays powerful and charismatic leaders, who, tasting supreme power, are tempted in the direction of tyranny and dictatorship. In Julius Caesar, Shakespeare shows Caesar becoming over-mighty, and Cassius tries to persuade his friend Brutus to take the lead, in opposition to dictatorship.

> (Brutus:) What means this shouting? I do fear, the people
> Choose Caesar for their king.
> (Cassius:) Ay, do you fear it?
> Then must I think you would not have it so.
> (Brutus:) I would not, Cassius; yet I love him well.

111

....

(Cassius:) I was born as free as Caesar; so were you:
We both have fed as well; and we can both
Endure the winter's cold as well as he…
            … And this man
Is now become a god; and Cassius is
A wretched creature, and must bend his body,
If Caesar carelessly but nod on him…
        … Ye gods, it doth amaze me
A man of such a feeble temper should
So get the start of the majestic world,
And bear the palm alone.   (Flourish and shout)
(Brutus:) Another general shout!
I do believe that these applauses are
For some new honours that are heaped on Caesar.
(Cassius:) Why, man, he doth bestride the narrow world
Like a Colossus, and we petty men
Walk under his huge legs and peep about
To find ourselves dishonourable graves.
Men at some time are masters of their fates:
The fault, dear Brutus, is not in our stars,
But in ourselves, that we are underlings.

      ....

Now, in the names of all the gods at once,
Upon what meat doth this our Caesar feed,
That he is grown so great? Age, thou art shamed!
Rome, thou hast lost the breed of noble bloods!
When went there by an age, since the great flood,
But it was famed with more than with one man?
When could they say, till now, that talked of Rome,
That her wide walls encompassed but one man?   (1.2.79)

Later plays rise to greater heights and contain deeper thoughts, sometimes obscured by compression of language, but here in Julius Caesar we see Shakespeare supreme in his command of words, which are direct, clear and full of imagery. The image in this passage is of course the Colossus of Rhodes, the huge statue that in ancient times was said to bridge the entrance to the harbor at Rhodes so that ships in full sail could pass under the legs.

Dictators always have a fear of rivals who would unseat them, and Caesar is no exception:

(Caesar:) Let me have men about me that are fat;
Sleek-headed men, and such as sleep o' nights;
Yond Cassius has a lean and hungry look;
He thinks too much: such men are dangerous.
(Antony:) Fear him not, Caesar: he's not dangerous;
He is a noble Roman, and well given.   (=disposed)
(Caesar:) Would he were fatter! – but I fear him not:
Yet if my name were liable to fear,
I do not know the man I should avoid
So soon as that spare Cassius. He reads much;
He is a great observer, and looks
Quite through the deeds of men; he loves no plays,
As thou dost, Antony; he hears no music:
Seldom he smiles, and smiles in such a sort
As if he mocked himself, and scorned his spirit
That could be moved to smile at any thing.
Such men as he be never at heart's ease
Whiles they behold a greater than themselves,
And therefore are they very dangerous.
I rather tell thee what is to be feared
Than what I fear; for always I am Caesar.
Come on my right hand, for this ear is deaf,
And tell me truly what thou think'st of him.   (1.2.191)

That last sentence is irrelevant to the action of the play, but is typical of the small touches of real life that can help to fill out Shakespeare's characters and make them credible human beings. Much of this passage comes directly from North's Plutarch:

> Caesar also had Cassius in great jealousy, and suspected him much: whereupon he said on a time to his friends, 'What will Cassius do, think ye? I like not his pale looks.' Another time when Caesar's friends complained unto him of Antonius and Dolabella, that they pretended some mischief towards him: he answered them again, "As for those fat men and smooth-combed heads," quoth he, "I never reckon of them; but these pale-visaged and carrion-lean people, I fear them most," meaning Brutus and Cassius.

Shakespeare has drawn on Plutarch's account but we must admire how, 'in the quick forge and working house of thought', he has enlarged the character of Cassius to make him similar to people we all have known. As the play progresses we see that he has more common sense and a better judgment than Brutus, who although the real hero of the play, is too much of an idealist to make wise decisions, and surely the decision to stab his friend was not an action that goes with a noble mind. One motive that drove him to lead the conspirators was his claim (alluded to in the play) that he was descended from Lucius Junius Brutus, who expelled the last king from Rome and became one of the first pair of consuls in 509 BC.

It was the thought of Caesar being offered a kingly crown that enraged the conspirators, and Shakespeare describes the scene vividly and even humorously through the mouth of cynical Casca:

(Casca:) there was a crown offered him; and being offered him, he put it by with the back of his hand, thus; and then the people fell a-shouting.

(Brutus:) What was the second noise for?

(Casca:) Why, for that too.

(Cassius:) They shouted thrice: what was the last cry for?

(Casca:) Why, for that too.

(Brytus:) Was the crown offered him thrice?

(Casca:) Ay, marry, was't, and he put it by thrice, every time gentler than other; and at every putting-by mine honest neighbours shouted.

(Cassius:) Who offered him the crown?

(Casca:) Why, Antony.

(Brutus:) Tell us the manner of it, gentle Casca.

(Casca:) I can as well be hanged as tell the manner of it: It was mere foolery; I did not mark it. I saw Mark Antony offer him a crown; yet 'twas not a crown neither, 'twas one of these coronets; and, as I told you, he put it by once; but for all that, to my thinking, he would fain have had it. Then he offered it to him again; then he put it by again; but to my thinking, he was very loath to lay his fingers off it. And then he offered it the third time. He put it the third time by; and still as he refused it, the rabblement hooted, and clapped their chopt hands, and threw up their sweaty night-caps, and uttered such a deal of stinking breath because Caesar refused the crown, that it had almost choked Caesar; for he swounded, and fell down at it. And for mine own part, I durst not laugh, for fear of opening my lips and receiving the bad air.

(Cassius:) But soft, I pray you: what, did Caesar swound?

(Casca:) He fell down in the market-place, and foamed at the mouth, and was speechless.

(Brutus:) 'Tis very like; he hath the falling-sickness.   (=epilepsy)

(Cassius:) No, Caesar hath it not; but you and I, and honest Casca, we have the falling sickness.

(Casca continues:) … When he came to himself again, he said, if he had done or said anything amiss, he desired their worships to think it was his infirmity. Three or four wenches, where I stood, cried, "Alas, good soul," and forgave him with all their hearts; but there's no heed to be taken of them; if Caesar had stabbed their mothers, they would have done no less.   (1.2.219)

(Casca again, a little later in the play:)

they say the senators tomorrow
Mean to establish Caesar as a king;
And he shall wear his crown by sea and land,
In every place, save here in Italy.

(Cassius:) I know where I will wear this dagger then;
Cassius from bondage will deliver Cassius…

(Casca:)   … So can I:
So every bondman in his own hand bears
The power to cancel his captivity.   (1.3.85)

Even though it may have no bearing on the action, Shakespeare cannot resist adding small touches which help to create a convincing human being, and there is an example in this scene:

(Casca:) Stand close awhile, for here comes one in haste.

(Cassius:) 'Tis Cinna. I do know him by his gait.   (1.3.131)

How often have we recognised a friend in the distance by his unique manner of walking.

In a soliloquy, Brutus weighs the momentous issues in his mind:

It must be by his death: and for my part,
I know no personal cause to spurn at him,
But for the general. He would be crowned: (general good)
How that might change his nature, there's the question.
It is the bright day that brings forth the adder,
And that craves wary walking. Crown him? – that; –
And then, I grant, we put a sting in him,   (sting of adder)
That at his will he may do danger with.

Th'abuse of greatness is when it disjoins
Remorse from power; and, to speak truth of Caesar,
I have not known when his affections swayed   (=feelings)
More than his reason. But 'tis a common proof,
That lowliness is young ambitions ladder,
Whereto the climber-upward turns his face;
But when he once attains the upmost round,
He then unto the ladder turns his back,
Looks in the clouds, scorning the base degrees
By which he did ascend. So Caesar may…
… And therefore think him as a serpent's egg,
Which, hatched, would, as his kind, grow mischievous,
And kill him in the shell.   (2.1.10)

The master of imaginative metaphor provides us with lines that stay in the memory: "It is the bright day that brings forth the adder, and that craves wary walking." The disjoining of remorse from power carries even more significance when we learn that 'remorse' in Elizabethan usage conveyed the meaning of 'compassion'. Cassius arranges for messages to be thrown in at Brutus' window, purporting to come from ordinary citizens, urging him to act:

(Brutus opens the letter, and reads:)
'Brutus, thou sleep'st; awake, and see thyself'
'Shall Rome, etc. Speak, strike, redress! … '
'Brutus, thou sleep'st; awake!'
Such instigations have been often dropped
Where I have took them up.
'Shall Rome, etc.' Thus must I piece it out:
Shall Rome stand under one man's awe? What, Rome?
My ancestors did from the streets of Rome
The Tarquin drive, when he was called a king.
'Speak, strike, redress!' Am I entreated
To speak, and strike? O Rome, I make thee promise,
If the redress will follow, thou receivest
Thy full petition at the hand of Brutus.   (2.1.46)

This speech contains the crux of the argument whether or not to assassinate a tyrant: will it lead to the redress of wrongs? Will a better society automatically follow?

The conspirators go to meet Caesar, to conduct him to the Senate

House. Here is a moment of 'dramatic irony' when the audience knows the threat to Caesar's life, but he himself does not:

> Good friends, go in, and taste some wine with me;
> And we, like friends, will straightway go together. (2.2.126)

Plutarch records that "one Artemidorus, . . a doctor of rhetoric in the Greek tongue, who by means of his profession was very familiar with certain of Brutus' confederates, and therefore knew the most part of all their practices against Caesar, came and brought him a little bill, written with his own hand, of all that he meant to tell him. ... Caesar took it of him, but could never read it, though he many times attempted it, for the number of people that did salute him: but holding it still in his hand, keeping it to himself, went on withal into the Senate-house." (Life of Caesar)

Shakespeare seizes upon this episode, and imagines the contents of the 'bill'. He does not simply list the conspirators, but gives each name its own unique phrase, couched in sonorous and alliterative language, the whole conveying a mortal threat:

> Caesar, beware of Brutus; take heed of Cassius; come not near Casca; have an eye to Cinna; trust not Trebonius; mark well Metellus Cimber; Decius Brutus loves thee not; thou hast wronged Caius Ligarius. There is but one mind in all these men, and it is bent against Caesar. If thou beest not immortal, look about you: security gives way to conspiracy. The mighty gods defend thee! Thy lover, Artemidorus. (2.3.1)

"There is but one mind in all these men, and it is bent against Caesar." Listen to the repeated 'n's and 'm's and the gradual rising vowels in the accented words: 'but one mind' -'men' -'bent against'. A translation error changed Plutarch's *Decimus* Brutus into Decius. As Caesar and the conspirators enter the Senate there is a tense moment, which seems to be an invention of Shakespeare's own creation:

> (Popilius:) I wish your enterprise today may thrive.
> (Cassius:) What enterprise, Popilius?
> (Popilius:)   Fare you well.
>   (leaves Cassius and joins Caesar)
> (Brutus:) What said Popilius Lena?
> (Cassius:) He wished today our enterprise might thrive.
> I fear our purpose is discovered.
> (Brutus:) Look how he makes to Caesar: mark him.
> (Cassius:) Casca, be sudden, for we fear prevention. (prevent=forestall)
> Brutus, what shall be done? If this be known,

117

Cassius or Caesar never shall turn back,
For I will slay myself.
(Brutus:) Cassius, be constant:
Popilius Lena speaks not of our purposes;
For look, he smiles, and Caesar doth not change.   (2.3.13)

The immediate pretext for the assassination of Caesar is his refusal to grant Metellus Cimber's appeal for his brother's banishment to be revoked. This is an opportunity for Shakespeare to show the inflexible arrogance of the dictator. In passing, it is interesting to note that the word 'assassination' was first introduced into the language by Shakespeare.

(Cassius:) Pardon, Caesar; Caesar, pardon:
As low as to thy foot doth Cassius fall,
To beg enfranchisement for Publius Cimber,
(Caesar:) I could well be moved, if I were as you;
If I could pray to move, prayers would move me;
But I am constant as the northern star,
Of whose true-fixed and resting quality
There is no fellow in the firmament.
The skies are painted with unnumbered sparks,
They are all fire, and every one doth shine;
But there's but one in all doth hold his place.
So in the world: 'tis furnished well with men:
And men are flesh and blood, and apprehensive;   (capable of
Yet in the number I do know but one   apprehending)
That unassailable holds on his rank,
Unshaked of motion; and that I am he,
Let me a little show it, even in this,
That I was constant Cimber should be banished,
And constant do remain to keep him so.
(Cinna:) O Caesar –
(Caesar:)   Hence! Wilt thou lift up Olympus?
(Decius:) Great Caesar –
(Caesar:)   Doth not Brutus bootless kneel?   (i.e. in vain)
(Casca:) Speak, hands, for me!(They stab Caesar)
(Caesar:) Et tu, Brutè? – Then fall, Caesar!   (Dies)
(Cinna:) Liberty! Freedom! Tyranny is dead!
Run hence, proclaim, cry it about the streets.
(Cassius:) Some to the common pulpits, and cry out,
"Liberty, freedom, and enfranchisement!"   (3.1.55)

118

Of course, it is obvious to any student of history that liberty and freedom do not automatically follow such a political murder, and Shakespeare makes that point in the course of the rest of the play. A political vacuum attracts ambitious adventurers, and we look on as Antony and Octavius (later the Emperor Augustus) seize the vacant centre of power. Shakespeare had already explored the period of civil strife which followed on the murders of Richard the Second and Henry the Sixth. The reader can no doubt think of other examples in history where revolutions have not led to 'liberty, equality and fraternity', but directly to new forms of despotism.

After the assassination of Caesar, the conspirators indulge in the gruesome ritual of dipping their hands in Caesar's blood. This episode is not mentioned in the histories, and seems to spring from the dramatist's imagination, and certainly it gives him an opportunity for some magnificent lines, with the Globe in mind:

> (Cassius:)   How many ages hence
> Shall this our lofty scene be acted o'er,
> In states unborn, and accents yet unknown!   (3.1.111)

That last line gives me an excuse to focus on the United States, with its distinctive accent, and to draw attention to a performance of Julius Caesar in the Fall of 1864, when three brothers took part, members of a distinguished acting family. The brothers were Edwin Booth, Junius Brutus Booth – note the name – and John Wilkes Booth. The latter was a supporter of the Confederacy, and, bitter after its defeat, he forced his way into the President's box at Ford's Theatre, Washington, on April 14, 1865, and fatally shot Abraham Lincoln in the back of the head, then leaping down to the stage shouted: Sic Semper Tyrannis – 'thus always to tyrants'- the motto of South Carolina, the first state to secede from the Union. We can only guess that the misguided man was acting out the 'lofty scene' of Caesar's murder.

Antony, in a soliloquy over Caesar's corpse, forecasts the further bloodshed which will follow the assassination:

> O, pardon me, thou bleeding piece of earth,
> That I am meek and gentle with these butchers.
> Thou art the ruins of the noblest man
> That ever livèd in the tide of times.
> Woe to the hand that shed this costly blood!
> Over thy wounds now do I prophesy …
> … A curse shall light upon the limbs of men;

119

> Domestic fury and fierce civil strife
> Shall cumber all the parts of Italy;
> Blood and destruction shall be so in use,
> And dreadful objects so familiar,
> That mothers shall but smile when they behold
> Their infants quartered with the hands of war,
> All pity choked with custom of fell deeds;
> And Caesar's spirit, ranging for revenge,
> With Até by his side come hot from hell,   (goddess of mischief)
> Shall in these confines with a monarch's voice
> Cry 'Havoc!' and let slip the dogs of war,
> That this foul deed shall smell above the earth
> With carrion men, groaning for burial.   (3.1.254)

'The dogs of war' reminds us of the Prologue to Henry the Fifth, when we are invited to imagine 'the warlike Harry' and 'at his heels, leashed in like hounds, should famine, sword, and fire crouch for employment.' The first couple of lines of Antony's soliloquy are brilliantly effective not only because of the use of an original and arresting metaphor, but also because after hearing a succession of pleasant 'ee' vowels, the mood is abruptly shattered with the brutal 'butchers.'

So far this chapter has followed Shakespeare's theme that order and strong leadership are essential ingredients of a stable society. What has emerged also is his fear of the two extremes of weak leadership on the one hand, and despotism on the other. Three centuries before universal franchise and the ballot box, it is also clear that he feared rule by the mob. His play Coriolanus contrasts the arrogance of the powerful leader with the fickleness of the common people who are able to unseat him. He had read his Plutarch thoroughly, and may have adopted the maxim he found there that 'it is a virtue of the mind which teacheth a man the mean point, between the two faulty extremities of too much and too little, wherein the commendation of all doings consisteth.'

In Julius Caesar we see how the speeches of Brutus and then of Antony sway the common people, now one way, now the other. First, from Brutus' speech: (3.2.18)

> If there be any in this assembly, any dear friend of Caesar's, to
> him I say that Brutus' love to Caesar was no less than his. If then
> that friend demand why Brutus rose against Caesar, this is my
> answer: not that I loved Caesar less, but that I loved Rome more.
> Had you rather that Caesar were living, and die all slaves, than

that Caesar were dead, to live all free men? ... Who is here so base, that would be a bondman? If any, speak; for him I have offended. Who is here so vile, that will not love his country? If any, speak; for him have I offended.

After his speech, members of the crowd come out with approving words
    Bring him with triumph home unto his house.
    Give him a statue with his ancestors.
And the irrational, unconsciously ironic:
    Let him be Caesar.
Contemplating the man that has been slain:
    This Caesar was a tyrant.
               - Nay, that's certain.
    We are blest that Rome is rid of him.

Then Antony speaks, and subtly and deviously moves the plebeians in the opposite direction. In Plutarch's Life of Antonius he records that Antony:
    ... made a funeral oration in commendation of Caesar, according to the ancient custom of praising noble men at their funerals. When he saw that the people were very glad and desirous also to hear Caesar spoken of, and his praises uttered, he mingled his oration with lamentable words; and by amplifying of matters did greatly move their hearts and affections unto pity and compassion. In fine, to conclude his oration, he unfolded before the whole assembly the bloody garments of the dead, thrust through in many places with their swords, and called the malefactors cruel and cursed murtherers. With these words he put the people into such a fury, that they presently took Caesar's body, and burnt it in the market-place, with such tables and forms as they could get together. Then when the fire was kindled, they took firebrands, and ran to the murtherers' houses to set them on fire...

Shakespeare took Plutarch's account of Antony's speech, applied his imaginative mind to it, and created one of the most memorable passages in the whole play. I say memorable, for I had to memorise it at school, and much of it has stayed in the memory for 70 years. The speech is far too long to reproduce here, but some passages deserve notice. As Antony gradually undermines the conspirators, he is careful to appear to respect them by repeated references to them as 'honourable men', a phrase which towards the end becomes a mocking sneer. These lines especially show how cleverly Antony works on the emotions of the crowd:

> You all did love him once, not without cause;
> What cause withholds you then to mourn for him?
> O judgment, thou art fled to brutish beasts,
> And men have lost their reason. Bear with me.
> My heart is in the coffin there with Caesar,
> And I must pause till it come back to me.   (3.2.108)

One of the plebeians guesses the outcome, true of most political assassinations:

> I fear there will be a worse come in his place.

The sonorous rhythm of this line could not be improved upon:

> If you have tears, prepare to shed them now.   (3.2.174)

After Antony has worked the crowd up to fever pitch, how ironical are his self-deprecating lines, with their hammering monosyllabic words:

> I am no orator, as Brutus is,
> But, as you know me all, a plain blunt man,
> That love my friend; and that they know full well
> That gave me public leave to speak of him.
> For I have neither wit, nor words, nor worth,
> Action, nor utterance, nor the power of speech
> To stir men's blood; I can only speak right on.   (3.2.221)

The mob go on the rampage, and Shakespeare's contempt for such ignorant and lawless behaviour comes out in his account of the fate of poor Cinna the poet, an account not without its humorous side:

> (1st Plebeian:) What is your name?
> (2nd Pleb:) Whither are you going?
> (3rd Pleb:) Where do you dwell?
> (4th Pleb:) Are you a married man or a bachelor?
> (2nd Pleb:) Answer every man directly.
> (1st Pleb:) Ay, and briefly.
> (4th Pleb:) Ay, and wisely.
> (3rd Pleb:) Ay, and truly, you were best.
> (Cinna:) What is my name? Whither am I going? Where do I
> dwell? Am I a married man or a bachelor? Then, to answer every

man directly and briefly, wisely and truly: wisely I say, I am a bachelor.

(2nd Pleb:) That's as much as to say they are fools that marry. You'll bear me a bang for that, I fear. Proceed, directly.

(Cinna:) Directly, I am going to Caesar's funeral.

(1st Pleb:) As a friend or an enemy?

(Cinna:) As a friend.

(2nd Pleb:) The matter is answered directly.

For your dwelling, briefly.

(Cinna:) Briefly, I dwell by the Capitol.

(3rd Pleb:) Your name, sir, truly.

(Cinna:) Truly, my name is Cinna.

(1st Pleb:) Tear him to pieces! He's a conspirator.

(Cinna:) I am Cinna the poet. I am Cinna the poet.

(4th Pleb:) Tear him for his bad verses, tear him for his bad verses.

(Cinna:) I am not Cinna the conspirator.

(1st Pleb:) It is no matter, his name's Cinna; pluck but his name out of his heart, and turn him going.

(3rd Pleb:) Tear him, tear him! Come, brands, ho! Firebrands! To Brutus', to Cassius'; burn all! Some to Decius' house, and some to Casca's; some to Ligarius'. Away! go! (3.3.5)

After Caesar's death, the new strong men waste no time, but proceed to eliminate their rivals for power in the manner characteristic of dictators throughout the ages:

(Antony:) These many then shall die; their names are pricked.

(Octavius:) Your brother too must die; consent you, Lepidus?

(Lepidus:) I do consent –

(Octavius:) Prick him down, Antony.

(Lepidus:) - Upon condition Publius shall not live,

Who is your sister's son, Mark Antony.

(Antony:) He shall not live. Look, with a spot I damn him. (4.1.1)

There is so much more in that play, but I leave it with regret, in order to return to the theme of this chapter, the organization of the state and the exercise of power. This leads us naturally to another of Shakespeare's Roman plays, Coriolanus. In that play the dramatist seems to be fascinated by the clash of two extremes. On the one hand is Caius Martius, later called Coriolanus, who is carried away by his own powers of command and sense of destiny, and on the other hand the changeable multitude, now for Coriolanus, now against him. They have grievances, outlined in these extracts from North's Plutarch:

> ... there grew sedition in the city, because the Senate did favour the rich against the people, who did complain of the sore oppression of usurers, of whom they borrowed money. For those that had little, were yet spoiled of that little they had by their creditors, for lack of ability to pay the usury: who offered their goods to be sold, to them that would give most. And such as had nothing left, their bodies were laid hold of, and they were made their bond men, notwithstanding all the wounds and cuts they showed, which they had received in many battles, fighting for defence of their country and commonwealth...
>
> (when) ... that the Senate would give no ear to them ... and suffered them to be made slaves and bond men to their creditors, and besides, to be turned out of all that ever they had: they fell then even to flat rebellion and mutiny, and to stir up dangerous tumults within the city.

Plutarch goes on to record that Martius was strongly in favour of using force to suppress this mutiny.

In Shakespeare's version of events, the main cause of grievance is the failure of crops and consequent shortage of grain. The play has been dated to about 1607-8, and he and his audience would have had fresh in mind various risings in the Midlands during 1607 and 1608, protesting at the shortage of food, and it is known that during 1608-9 the government spent £2,000,000 on the import of corn to alleviate distress. The play may also be dated by a reference to a 'coal of fire upon the ice.' The winter of 1607-8 was exceptionally severe, and the Thames froze over for the first time since 1564-5. Booths were set up 'standing upon the ice, as fruitsellers, victuallers, that sold beere and wine, shoe makers and a barber's tent,' and some were 'ready with pans of coals to warm your fingers'. In the museum at the Globe Theatre there is a fascinating model which shows a fair taking place on the frozen Thames.

Coriolanus begins with 'a company of mutinous citizens, with staves, clubs, and other weapons.'

> (First Citizen:) Before we proceed any further, hear me speak.
> (All:) Speak, speak.
> (First Cit:) You are all resolved rather to die than to famish?
> (All:) Resolved, resolved.
> (First Cit:) First, you know Caius Martius is chief enemy to the people.

124

(All:) We know't, we know't.

(First Cit:) Let us kill him, and we'll have corn at our own price. Is't a verdict?

(All:) No more talking on't; let it be done. Away, away!

(Second Cit:) One word, good citizens.

(First Cit:) We are accounted poor citizens, the patricians good. What authority surfeits on would relieve us. If they would yield us but the superfluity while it were wholesome, we might guess they relieved us humanely; but they think we are too dear: the leanness that afflicts us, the object of our misery is as an inventory to particularize their abundance; our sufferance is a gain to them. Let us revenge this with our pikes, ere we become rakes. For the gods know, I speak this in hunger for bread, not in thirst for revenge. (1.1.1)

According to Plutarch, the Senate 'did send unto them certain of the pleasantest old men, and the most acceptable to the people' and 'the chief man of the message from the Senate' was Menenius Agrippa.

(Second Cit:) Worthy Menenius Agrippa, one that hath always loved the people.

(First Cit:) He's one honest enough, would all the rest were so!

(Menenius:) What work's, my countrymen, in hand? Where go you with bats and clubs? The matter? Speak, I pray you.

(First Cit:) Our business is not unknown to th'Senate; they have had inkling this fortnight what we intend to do, which now we'll show 'em in deeds…

(Men:) Why masters, my good friends, mine honest neighbours, will you undo yourselves?

(First Cit:) We cannot, sir, we are undone already.

(Men:) I tell you, friends, most charitable care
Have the patricians of you. For your wants,
Your suffering in this dearth, you may as well
Strike at the heaven with your staves, as lift them
Against the Roman state, whose course will on
The way it takes, cracking ten thousand curbs
Of more strong link asunder than can ever
Appear in your impediment. For the dearth,
The gods, not the patricians, make it, and
Your knees to them, not arms, must help. Alack,
You are transported by calamity

Thither where more attends you; and you slander
The helms o'th'state, who care for you like fathers,
When you curse them as enemies
(First Citizen:) Care for us? True indeed! They ne'er cared for
us yet. Suffer us to famish, and their storehouses crammed with
grain; make edicts for usury, to support usurers; repeal daily any
wholesome act established against the rich, and provide more
piercing statutes daily, to chain up and restrain the poor. If the
wars eat us not up, they will; and there's all the love they bear
us.   (1.1.54)

Shakespeare, as usual, can see both sides of the argument. Coleridge
discerned in this play "the wonderful philosophic impartiality of Shakespeare's politics." He no doubt knew Aristotle's dictum that right government must be for the good of all its citizens. Nevertheless, as one of
the wealthy landowners of Stratford, it is likely he would have taken their
side when the farm labourers of Warwickshire rose in 1607-8. They were
protesting partly at the enclosures made by landowners which turned
arable into more profitable pasture, thereby taking away the labourers'
means of livelihood and reducing the local output of corn. This chimes
in with North's Plutarch:

> Now when this war was ended, the flatterers of the people began
> to stir up sedition again... For they did ground this second in-
> surrection against the nobility and patricians, upon the people's
> misery and misfortune... Because the most part of the arable
> land within the territory of Rome was become heathy and barren
> for lack of ploughing, for that they had no time nor mean to cause
> corn to be brought them out of other countries to sow, by reason
> of their wars, which made the extreme dearth they had among
> them.

One line in this account could apply to the world's famine areas today:
> ... though there had been plenty enough, yet the common people
> had no money to buy it.

At the start of this chapter we mentioned the parallel that age saw
between the interaction of the various parts of the human body and the
interaction between the various social classes that make up the body of
the state. Plutarch relates that Menenius used the same metaphor to try
to placate the mutinous citizens, and Shakespeare made use of it.

(Menenius: I shall tell you
A pretty tale; it may be you have heard it…
There was a time, when all the body's members
Rebelled against the belly; thus accused it:
That only like a gulf it did remain
I'th'midst o'th'body, idle and unactive,
Still cupboarding the viand, never bearing
Like labour with the rest, where th'other instruments
Did see, and hear. Devise, instruct, walk, feel,
And, mutually participate, did minister
Unto the appetite and affection common
Of the whole body. The belly answered…
…   it tauntingly replied
To th'discontented members, the mutinous parts
That envied his receipt; even so most fitly,   (=what he received)
As you malign our senators, for that
They are not such as you…
The kingly crownèd head, the vigilant eye,
The counsellor heart, the arm our soldier,
Our steed the leg, the tongue our trumpeter,
With other muniments and petty helps   (m=supports)
In this our fabric…
          … if they did complain,
What could the belly answer? …
'True is it, my incorporate friends, 'quoth he,
'That I receive the general food at first
Which you do live upon; and fit it is,
Because I am the store-house and the shop
Of the whole body. But, if you do remember,
I send it through the rivers of your blood
Even to the court, the heart, to th'seat o'th'brain;
And through the cranks and offices of man,   (c=winding alleys?)
The strongest nerves and small inferior veins
From me receive that natural competency
Whereby they live… '
… The senators of Rome are this good belly,
And you the mutinous members; for examine
Their counsels and their cares, digest things rightly
Touching the weal o'th'common, you shall find
No public benefit which you receive

But it proceeds or comes from them to you,
And no way from yourselves.   (1.1.88)

At this distance we may ridicule the idea of a society where each citizen has an immutable rank from which he must not budge: the philosophy that all things are bright and beautiful, and

>The rich man in his castle,
>The poor man at his gate,
>God made them, high or lowly,
>And ordered their estate.

Shakespeare must have seen that the body of society was creaking at the joints: there was widespread unemployment and thousands of vagrants wandering about the country, searching for work or the means of basic survival. That led to the Poor Law of 1601, which laid a duty on parishes to relieve local poverty, and that indeed may be referred to as the 'public benefit which you receive.' As we know from many passages in the plays, Shakespeare's generous sympathy is always aroused by the sight of poverty and economic injustice, as these lines from Pericles demonstrate:

>(Third Fisherman:) I marvel how the fishes live in the sea.
>(First Fisherman:) Why, as men do a-land: the great ones eat up the little ones; I can compare our rich misers to nothing so fitly as to a whale; a' plays and tumbles, driving the poor fry before him, and at last devours them all at a mouthful. Such whales have I heard on o' the land, who never leave gaping till they've swallowed the whole parish, church, steeple, bells, and all.   (2.1.29)

A similar indignation concerning the injustice in the world is expressed in a passage from the Rape of Lucrece. For the word 'opportunity' we may interpret 'opportunism', selfish behaviour on the part of those in a position to do good:

>O Opportunity, thy guilt is great!
>'Tis thou that executest the traitor's treason;
>Thou sett'st the wolf where he the lamb may get;
>... When wilt thou be the humble suppliant's friend,
>And bring him where his suit may be obtained?
>When wilt thou sort an hour great strifes to end?
>Or free that soul which wretchedness hath chained?
>Give physic to the sick, ease to the pained?

128

The poor, lame, blind, halt, creep, cry out for thee;
But they ne'er meet with Opportunity.

The patient dies while the physician sleeps;
The orphan pines while the oppressor feeds;
Justice is feasting while the widow weeps;
Advice is sporting while infection breeds;
Thou grant'st no time for charitable deeds. (876)

That theme crops up again later in this book, but meanwhile there is more to explore in Coriolanus.

Menenius is an attractive and sympathetic character. Among many good lines given to him I select these, addressed to the devious tribunes:

You talk of pride. O that you could turn your eyes toward the napes of your necks, and make but an interior survey of your good selves. O that you could! (2.1.37)

It is a pity that Shakespeare could not have made a play about the worthy and wise Menenius, but he had to follow Plutarch, and so we are left with ice-cold Coriolanus, who, apart from the fact that he is a stubborn and fearless warrior – and the world has too many of them – and that he respects his mother, he has not one single redeeming virtue to which we may warm. Even the character of blood-soaked Macbeth interests us more. Shakespeare has constructed a competent and fast-moving drama, but one has the feeling that his heart was not in it.

After Caius Martius has led the Romans to victory against the Volscians in their city Corioli, he is given the title Coriolanus, and the senators wish to reward him by making him a consul. However, by the democratic custom of Rome, the appointment has also to win the approval of the common people, but Coriolanus despises them so vehemently that he cannot bring himself to stoop and ask for their support. Here, Shakespeare has an opportunity to show the fickleness of 'public opinion', cheering a leader (politician?) one minute, and cursing him the next.

(Enter two officers, to lay cushions in the Capitol)
(First Off:) Come, come, they are almost here. How many stand for consulships?
(Second Off:) Three, they say; but 'tis thought of everyone Coriolanus will carry it.
(First Off:) That's a brave fellow; but he's vengeance proud, and loves not the common people.

129

(Second Off:) 'Faith, there have been many great men that have flattered the people, who ne'er loved them; and there be many that they have loved, they know what wherefore: so that if they love they know not why, they hate upon no better a ground. (2.2.1)

The citizens at first support the granting of the consulship, but then, persuaded by their tribunes that Coriolanus continued to despise them, they change their minds. Coriolanus calls this a

          plot
To curb the will of the nobility:
Suffer't, and live with such as cannot rule,
Nor ever will be ruled.

Later in this scene he pursues the same theme:

              This double worship
Where one part does disdain with cause, the other
Insult without all reason: where gentry, title, wisdom,
Cannot conclude but by the yea and no
Of general ignorance, it must omit
Real necessities, and give way the while
To unstable slightness. Purpose so barr'd, it follows
Nothing is done to purpose...
...   Your dishonour
Mangles true judgement, and bereaves the state
Of that integrity which should becom't,
Not having the power to do the good it would
For th'ill which doth control't. (3.1.37)

The debate whether those in the lower ranks of society should have a say in the government has continued down to recent times. The argument raged on both sides when Disraeli's 1867 Reform Act gave the vote to working-class householders in the towns. Even Lord Derby, introducing the Bill, called it 'a leap in the dark.' After the Act became law, Robert Lowe, an opponent, said that now 'we must educate our masters.' Thomas Carlyle feared 'new supplies of blockheadism, gullilbility, bribeability, amenability to beer and balderdash... ' The Radical J.S. Mill was apprehensive that there might result 'a governing majority of manual labourers.' In the event the working men voted in the main for middle-class and upper-class candidates, and society did not dissolve into anarchy, but carried on much as before, and Britain moved towards the zenith of its history.

Since the subject of this chapter is the government of the state, the later scenes of Shakespeare's play are no longer relevant, but we cannot omit the moment when Coriolanus is banished:

(Brutus:) There's no more to be said but he is banish'd,
As enemy to the people and his country.
It shall be so!
(All Plebeians:)   It shall be so, it shall be so!
(Coriolanus:) You common cry of curs! whose breath I hate
As reek o'th'rotten fens, whose loves I prize
As the dead carcasses of unburied men
That do corrupt my air: I banish you!
And here remain with your uncertainty!
Let every feeble rumour shake your hearts!
Your enemies, with nodding of their plumes,
Fan you into despair! Have the power still
To banish your defenders, till at length
Your ignorance – which finds not till it feels,
Making but reservation of yourselves,   (i.e. you alone unbanished)
Still your own foes – deliver you as most
Abated captives to some nation   (abated=beaten)
That won you without blows! Despising
For you the city, thus I turn my back.
There is a world elsewhere!   (He goes out) (3.3.115)

Towards the end of the play, Coriolanus and his army surround Rome and threaten to destroy it, and appeals for mercy are likely to fall on deaf ears. This extract emphasizes the implacable character of the man:

(Menenius:) This Martius is grown from man to dragon: he has wings: he's more than a creeping thing.
(Sicinius:) He loved his mother dearly.
(Menenius:) So did he me; and he no more remembers his mother now than an eight-year-old horse. The tartness of his face sours ripe grapes. When he walks, he moves like an engine (cannon on wheels) and the ground shrinks before his treading. He is able to pierce a corslet with his eye, talks like a knell, and his hum is a battery. (i.e. cannon-fire) He sits in his state as a thing made for Alexander. (i.e. statue) What he bids be done is finished with his bidding. He wants nothing of a god but eternity, and a heaven to throne in.
(Sicinius:) Yes, mercy, if you report him truly.
(Menenius:) I paint him in the character. Mark what mercy his

mother shall bring from him. There is no more mercy in him than there is milk in a male tiger. (Cor 5.4.12)

How the story of Coriolanus ends with a surprising turn of fortune is told in a later chapter. Meanwhile, we continue with the subject of ignorant mobs, dealt with elsewhere in Shakespeare's works. First, after the unrelieved seriousness of Coriolanus, we need some entertainment, and we get it in plenty in Shakespeare's version of Jack Cade's rebellion of 1450, in Henry the Sixth, Part 2:

(the scene is Blackheath)

(George Bevis:) Come, and get thee a sword, though made of a lath … I tell thee, Jack Cade the clothier means to dress the commonwealth, and turn it, and set a new nap upon it.

(John Holland:) So he had need, for 'tis threadbare. Well, I say it was never merry world in England since gentlemen came up.

(Geo:) O miserable age! virtue is not regarded in handicraftsmen.

(John:) The nobility think scorn to go in leather aprons.

(Geo:) Nay, more; the king's council are no good workmen.

(John:) True; and yet it is said, 'Labour in thy vocation:' which is as much to say as, let the magistrates be labouring men; and therefore should we be magistrates.

(Geo:) Thou has hit it; for there's no better sign of a brave mind than a hard hand…

(Drum. Enter Cade, Dick the butcher, Smith the weaver, and a sawyer, with infinite numbers.)

(Cade:) We John Cade, so termed of our supposed father –

(Dick, aside:) Or rather, of stealing a cade of herrings.   (cade=a barrel of 500 herring)

(Cade:) For our enemies shall fall before us, inspired with the spirit of putting down kings and princes, - Command silence.

(Dick:) Silence!

(Cade:) My father was a Mortimer –

(Dick, aside:) He was an honest man, and a good bricklayer.

(Cade:) My mother was a Plantagenet –

(Dick, aside:) I knew her well; she was a midwife.

(Cade:) My wife descended of the Lacies –

(Dick, aside:) She was, indeed, a pedlar's daughter, and sold many laces…

(Cade:) I am able to endure much.

132

(Dick, aside:) No question of that, for I have seen him whipped three market-days together...

(Cade:) Be brave, then; for your captain is brave, and vows reformation. There shall be in England seven halfpenny loaves sold for a penny; the three-hooped pot shall have ten hoops;

> (ref. to wooden drinking pots with hoops around –
> this would then treble the contents!)

and I will make it a felony to drink small beer. All the realm shall be in common, and in Cheapside shall my palfrey go to grass. And when I am king, - as king I will be, -

(All:) God save your majesty!

(Cade:) I thank you, good people: there shall be no money; all shall eat and drink on my score; and I will apparel them all in one livery, that they may agree like brothers, and worship me their lord.

(Dick:) The first thing we do, let's kill all the lawyers.

(Cade:) Nay, that I mean to do. Is not this a lamentable thing, that of the skin of an innocent lamb should be made parchment? that parchment, being scribbled o'er, should undo a man? Some say the bee stings; but I say, 'tis the bee's wax, for I did but seal once to a thing, and I was never mine own man since...   (4.2.1)

The taking of London by the rebels is a bloody business, but Shakespeare finds room for one more line of humour:

> (Cade:) Now is Mortimer lord of this city. And here, sitting upon London-stone, I charge and command that, of this city's cost, the pissing conduit runs nothing but claret wine this first year of our reign.   (4.6.1)
>
> (London Stone, still to be seen in Cannon Street, traditionally Roman.)

When the rebels are cornered, and pardon is offered to them, they forsake Cade, who scolds them:

> And you, base peasants, do ye believe him? will you needs be hanged with your pardons about your necks? ... I thought ye would never have given out these arms till you had recovered your ancient freedom; but you are all recreants and dastards, and delight to live in slavery to the nobility. Let them break your backs with burdens, take your houses over your heads, ravish your wives and daughters before your faces: for me, I will make shift for one, and so, God's curse light upon you all!   (4.8.22)

As the rebels waver between following him or the authority of the king's ambassadors, Cade says in disgust:

> 'Was ever feather so lightly blown to and fro as this multitude?'
>
> (4.8.58)

Of course all these speeches come from Shakespeare's imagination. According to historical record, admittedly scanty, the rising was not a rabble, but included many of the gentry. The rebels' manifesto, Complaint of the Commons of Kent, was a protest against the mismanagement of the government and the rising taxes to pay for the French wars, and it had popular support until the rebels began to loot and murder in London.

In Henry the Fourth, Part 2, Shakespeare once more shows his contempt for the vacillating and inconstant way the masses switch their support from leader to leader:

> The commonwealth is sick of their own choice;
> Their over-greedy love hath surfeited.
> A habitation giddy and unsure
> Hath he that buildeth on the vulgar heart.
> O thou fond many! with what loud applause   (fond=weak & foolish)
> Didst thou beat heaven with blessing Bolingbroke,
> Before he was what thou wouldst have him be!
> And being now trimmed in thine own desires,   (trimmed=dressed)
> Thou, beastly feeder, art so full of him
> That thou provok'st thyself to cast him up.
> So, so, thou common dog, didst thou disgorge
> Thy glutton bosom of the royal Richard;
> And now thou wouldst eat thy dead vomit up,
> And howl'st to find it. What trust is in these times?
> They that, when Richard lived, would have him die,
> Are now become enamoured on his grave.
> Thou that threw'st dust upon his goodly head,
> When through proud London he came sighing on
> After the admirèd heels of Bolingbroke,
> Cry'st now, 'O earth! yield us that king again,
> And take thou this!' O, thoughts of men accurst!
> Past and to come seem best; things present, worst.   (1.3.87)

An ignorant crowd is adept at spreading gossip and tittle-tattle:

> Rumour is a pipe
> Blown by surmises, jealousies, conjectures,

And of so easy and so plain a stop
That the blunt monster with uncounted heads,
The still discordant wavering multitude,
Can play upon it.

In the archives of the British Museum there was discovered a remarkable manuscript, which may throw light on Shakespeare's attitude to the
mob. The manuscript is known as the Book of Sir Thomas More, and is
in the form of a play based upon episodes in his life. It was apparently
written in the 1590s, and the first third of it dealt with the events of May
Day 1517, when the London mob rose in protest against the presence in
the city of Lombard traders, and the nasty riot that ensued caused it to be
remembered as Evil May Day. According to the play, the riot was quelled
by the persuasion of a speech addressed to the rioters by Sir Thomas More.
The play never reached the stage, for the Master of the Revels, Edmund
Tilney, sent the manuscript back with an appended note of censorship:
"Leave out the insurrection wholly and the cause thereof, and begin with
Sir Thomas More at the Mayor's sessions, with a report afterwards of his
good service done, as Shreve (sheriff) of London upon a mutiny against the
Lombards, only by a short report and not otherwise, at your perils."

Judging by handwriting, the play was the work of at least six writers.
Three of the manuscript pages are thought to be in Shakespeare's own
handwriting and certainly the language, humour, and generous spirit of
it is in accordance with his style. Another tell-tale link with Shakespeare
is the spelling peculiar to him, e.g. 'scilens' for silence.

The author protests at the hounding of the immigrants and the demand that they be expelled, ignorant prejudice still rampant today:

Imagine that you see the wretched strangers,
Their babies at their backs, and their poor luggage
Plodding to th'ports and coasts for transportation…

The lines of the manuscript which touch on immigration are examined in more detail in a later chapter. Here, it is more relevant to give the
author's attitude to mob rule:

Grant them removed, and grant that this your noise
Hath chid down all the majesty of England …
And that you sit as kings in your desires,
Authority quite silenced by your brawl …
What had you got? I'll tell you: you had taught
How insolence and strong hand should prevail,

How order should be quelled, and by this pattern
Not one of you should live an agèd man,
For other ruffians, as their fancies wrought,
With self-same hand, self reasons, and self right
Would shark on you, and men like ravenous fishes
Would feed on one another.

All law-abiding citizens would applaud those sentiments. The tricky and perennial question remains: at what point does one strike a balance between an ordered society and individual freedoms?

Finally, a warning to all who exercise power:

man, proud man,
Dressed in a little brief authority,
Most ignorant of what he's most assured, -
His glassy essence – like an angry ape   (glassy essence: perhaps
Plays such fantastic tricks before high heaven   'transparent essential
As make the angels weep.   inner self, soul')

                                      (MFM 2.2.117)

THE WHOLE MAN

'Man', in Shakespeare's world, is shorthand for 'humankind', and must be understood to include women as well as men. It would be impossibly clumsy to write "What a piece of work is a man-stroke-woman". However, it would be foolish to ignore the fact that women played a subordinate role in that age, even though it was named after and dominated by a female ruler.

Shakespeare has no illusions about man's capacity for the most cold-bloodied evil, and this is the theme of the great tragedies, and an important thread running through many of the history plays. Nevertheless it is clear that our author believed in the potential greatness latent in the human spirit, able to rise to the heights despite every obstacle.

This ideal of the whole man, the fulfilled human being, comes directly from the humanism of the Renaissance writers. They rediscovered Plato and read there "Man is the measure of all things". At the opening of the Fifteenth Century Leonardo Bruni wrote: "The liberal arts owe their name to the fact that they liberate man and make him master of himself in a free world of free spirits." These ideas were harmonized with the theological concept of man created by God to be at the centre of the universe, with nature subordinate to him. Man was still seen as a fallen creature, but nevertheless capable of salvation and elevation through the gift of freewill and acceptance of belief in the Christian revelation. But in fact Shakespeare has very little to say about Christian theology, though occasional passages show that he was familiar with it. We must remember that the horrors of the religious conflicts and controversies of the previous reign were still a vivid memory, and wise men avoided fanning the embers back into flame. A further reason why Shakespeare should not want to draw attention to his own personal religious outlook is that his mother's Catholic forebears had suffered persecution, and his own father is known to have been a closet Catholic. In any case, a royal proclamation of 1559 had warned licencers of plays –

> 'to permit none to be played wherein either matters of religion or the governance of the estate of the commonweal shall be handled or treated.'

The status of the ideal man in Renaissance thought may be seen in an extract from Count Hannibal Romei's Courtier's Academy (1546), and one may spot parallels in Hamlet:

> That most excellent and great God ...   in the end made man, being of all worldly creatures and the most miraculous. ...
>
> Whereupon, calling unto him he said: Live, O Adam, in what life pleaseth thee best and take unto thyself those gifts which thou esteemest most dear. From this so liberal a grant had our free will its original, so that it is in our power to live like a plant, a living creature, like a man, and lastly like an
> angel; for if a man addict himself only to feeding and nourishment he becometh a plant, if to things sensual he is a brute beast, if to things reasonable and civil he groweth a celestial creature; but if he exalt the beautiful gift of his mind to things invisible and divine he transformeth himself into an angel and, to conclude, becometh the son of God.

In Hamlet we have:

> What is a man,
> If his chief good and market of his time
> Be but to sleep and feed? A beast, no more.
> Sure he that made us with such large discourse,
> Looking before and after, gave us not
> That capability and godlike reason
> To fust in us unused.   (fust=become musty)
>
> (4.4.33)

At the risk of reading too much into a casual phrase, we may comment that 'looking before and after' is the essence of civilization, which looks back to the history and accumulated wisdom of the past as a guide to planning and organising the future. It is also the method by which science advances.

The extract quoted from the Courtier's Academy finds another parallel in Hamlet:

> What a piece of work is a man! how noble in reason ! how infinite in faculties! in form and moving, how express and admirable! in action how like an angel! in apprehension how like a god! the beauty of the world, the paragon of animals!   (2.2.323)

Another Renaissance author who defined the supreme potential in man was Giovanni Pico della Mirandola, writing in 1486:

Now the Highest Father, God the Architect ... longed for someone to reflect on the plan of so great a creation, to love its beauty, and to admire its magnitude. When, therefore, everything was completed ... he began at last to consider the creation of man. ... 'I have set you at the centre of the world, so that from there you may more easily survey whatever is in the world. We have made you neither heavenly nor earthly, neither mortal nor immortal, so that ... you may fashion yourself in whatever form you shall prefer' ... O highest and marvellous felicity of man! To him it is granted to be whatever he chooses, to whatever he wills.

Pico also makes the Creator say: "Thou mayst sink into a beast, and be born anew to the divine likeness", and Shakespeare explores those extremes in the great tragedies.

The character of the whole man, the ideal man, as we see it portrayed in the plays, includes a wealth of qualities. Among these are honesty, generosity, compassion, forgiveness, courage, and, perhaps encapsulating them all, a transparency or openness of character, and the following pages will expand on each of these themes.

Let us begin with references to *honesty* and *truth*:

> (Hamlet again:) to be honest, as this world goes, is to be one man
> picked out of ten thousand.   (2.2.179)

From All's Well That Ends Well:

> 'Tis not the many oaths that makes the truth,
> But the plain single vow that is vowed true   (4.2.21)

and from the same play:

> No legacy is so rich as honesty.   (3.5.13)

Polonius may be a 'tedious old fool', but there is sound sense in much of the advice he gives to his son Laertes as he is about to return to France:

> This above all: to thine own self be true,
> And it must follow, as the night the day,
> Thou canst not then be false to any man.   (1.3.78)

- -

Cressida asks Troilus: will you be true? and he replies -

> Who, I? alas, it is my vice, my fault:

139

> While others fish with craft for great opinion,
> I with great truth catch mere simplicity;
> Whilst some with cunning gild their copper crowns,
> With truth and plainness I do wear mine bare.
> Fear not my truth: the moral of my wit
> Is – plain and true; there's all the reach of it.   (T&C 4.4.101)

- -

Calphurnia, wife of Julius Caesar, fearful of mortal danger, tries to dissuade him from going to the Senate:

> Let me, upon my knee, prevail in this.
> (Caesar:) Mark Antony shall say I am not well;
> And, for thy humour, I will stay at home.   (Enter Decius)
> Here's Decius Brutus, he shall tell them so.
> (Decius:) Caesar, all hail! Good morrow, worthy Caesar:
> I come to fetch you to the senate-house.
> (Caesar:) And you are come in very happy time
> To bear my greeting to the senators,
> And tell them that I will not come today;
> Cannot, is false, and that I dare not, falser:
> I will not come today: tell them so, Decius.
> (Calphurnia:) Say he is sick.
> (Caesar:)   Shall Caesar send a lie?
> Have I in conquest stretched mine arm so far
> To be afeard to tell greybeards the truth?   (2.2.54)

- -

In case the emphasis on moral rectitude should become too priggish, Shakespeare can always be relied on to prick the bubble of pomposity. Here is the arch-rogue Autolycus, prepared to speak truth if it will serve his purpose:

> Though I am not naturally honest, I am so sometimes by chance.
> (WT 4.3.734)

And Autolycus again, tongue in cheek:

> Let me have no lying, it becomes none but tradesmen.   (WT 4.4.722)

- -

(hypocrisy)

Virtue stands out more clearly when contrasted against the dark background of its opposite. In the case of honesty we may judge how much it was prized by Shakespeare when we see, throughout the plays, that *deceit, hypocrisy* and hollow flattery are anathema to him. Here we have Hamlet in the graveyard, addressing Horatio:

> (Hamlet:) That skull had a tongue in it, and could sing once: how the knave jowls it to the ground as if 'twere Cain's jawbone, that did the first murder! This might be the pate of a politician ... or of a courtier; which could say, Good-morrow, sweet lord! How dost thou, good lord? This might be my lord such-a –one, that praised my lord such-a-one's horse, when he meant to beg it, might it not? (5.1.81)

That same play is a rich source of comment on integrity and its antithesis. Here, Hamlet says why he values the friendship of Horatio, and has a side-swipe at flattery:

> (Hamlet:) Horatio, thou art e'en as just a man
> As e'er my conversation coped withal.
> (Horatio:) O! my dear lord –
> (Hamlet:)   Nay, do not think I flatter;
> For what advancement may I hope from thee,
> That no revenue hast but thy good spirits
> To feed and clothe thee? Why should the poor be flattered?
> No; let the candied tongue lick absurd pomp,
> And crook the pregnant hinges of the knee
> Where thrift may follow fawning. Dost thou hear?
> Since my dear soul was mistress of her choice
> And could of men distinguish, her election
> Hath sealed thee for herself; for thou hast been
> As one, in suffering all, that suffers nothing,
> A man that Fortune's buffets and rewards
> Hast ta'en with equal thanks ...
>   ... Give me that man
> That is not passion's slave, and I will wear him
> In my heart's core, ay, in my heart of heart,
> As I do thee. (3.2.59)

Shakespeare's quick brain invented or adapted words to fit his train of thought, and in this passage he introduced 'candied' into the language, from an existing verb 'to candy' meaning 'cover with sugar,' a meaning still in current use in America.

    Deceit is a recurrent theme in **Macbeth**:
(Duncan:)   There's no art
To find the mind's construction in the face:
He was a gentleman on whom I built
An absolute trust.   (1.4.11)

- -

(Lady Macbeth to Macbeth:)
Your face, my thane, is as a book where men
May read strange matters: to beguile the time,
Look like the time; bear welcome in your eye,
Your hand, your tongue: look like the innocent flower,
But be the serpent under't.   (1.5.63)

- -

(Macbeth:) Away, and mock the time with fairest show:
False face must hide what the false heart doth know.   (1.7.81)

- -

(the porter of Macbeth's castle pretends he is porter at the gate of hell:)   (2.3.3)
              Knock, knock, knock. Who's there, I' the name of Beelzebub? ...   Faith, here's an equivocator, that could swear in both the scales against either scale; who committed treason enough for God's sake, yet could not equivocate to heaven: O, come in, equivocator. .. But this place is too cold for hell. I'll devil –porter it no further: I had thought to have let in some of all professions, that go the primrose way to the everlasting bonfire.

- -

(Malcolm:) To show an unfelt sorrow is an office
Which the false man does easy.
(and his brother Donalbain replies:) Where we are,
There's daggers in men's smiles.   (2.3.143)

(hypocrisy)

In Richard the Third, the scheming Duke of Gloucester, aiming for the throne, in pretending to be the pious soul of honesty sinks to the very depths of mendacity:

> Because I cannot flatter and speak fair,
> Smile in men's faces, smooth, deceive, and cog,   (=cheat)
> Duck with French nods and apish courtesy,
> I must be held a rancorous enemy.
> Cannot a plain man live, and think no harm,
> But thus his simple truth must be abused
> By silken, sly insinuating Jacks?   (1.3.47)

- -

After the death of Edward IV, his son Edward, the young Prince of Wales, heir to the throne, arrives in London from Ludlow:

> (Duke of Buckingham:)
> Welcome, sweet prince, to London, to your chamber.
> (Duke of Gloucester, uncle of the prince:)
> Welcome, dear cousin, my thoughts' sovereign;
> The weary way hath made you melancholy.
> (Prince:) No, uncle; but our crosses on the way
> Have made it tedious, wearisome, and heavy;
> I want more uncles here to welcome me.
> (Gloucester has imprisoned the missing uncles)
> (Gloucester:) Sweet prince, the untainted virtue of your years
> Hath not yet dived into the world's deceit:
> No more can you distinguish of a man
> Than of his outward show; which, God he knows,
> Seldom or never jumpeth with the heart.
> Those uncles which you want were dangerous;
> Your Grace attended to their sugared words,
> But looked not on the poison of their hearts:
> God keep you from them, and from such false friends!   (3.1.1)

Modern historians hasten to say that, in following Tudor propaganda, Shakespeare's portrayal of Richard III as a villain is grossly unfair. The real Richard was intelligent, courageous, generous, cultured, an able soldier and administrator. The History Today Companion to British History notes that "the instinct to leap to the defence of anyone who has

143

had the monumental misfortune to have their character assassinated by Shakespeare has resulted in Richard the Third becoming the most controversial of English kings." There still remains the unanswered question: did he order the murder of the Princes in the Tower?

The Tragedy of Othello, one of the fastest-moving of the plays, with scarcely a superfluous word, shows us the stark contrast between the frank, trusting, honest man and the devious, honest-seeming villain. Iago, eaten up with envy of his great general, admits:

> The Moor is of a free and open nature
> That thinks men honest that but seem to be so
> And will as tenderly be led by the nose
> As asses are.   (1.3.303)

The audience is aghast as they watch Iago spin his monstrous web of lies to bring ruin to Othello, who in his blindness repeatedly refers to his subordinate as 'honest Iago'. Shakespeare's extraordinary imagination creates the towering figure of Othello with his flawed nobility, a character convincingly conveyed in the dignity of his final speech:

> Soft you: a word before you go
> I have done the state some service and they know't;
> No more of that. I pray you, in your letters,
> When you shall these unlucky deeds relate,   (unlucky=
> Speak of me as I am; nothing extenuate,   ill-omened,disastrous)
> Nor set down aught in malice. Then must you speak
> Of one that loved not wisely but too well;
> Of one, not easily jealous, but, being wrought,
> Perplexed in the extreme; of one whose hand,
> Like the base Indian, threw a pearl away
> Richer than all his tribe.   (5.2.334)

The central theme running through Measure For Measure is the exposure of hypocrisy. Angelo, the temporary governor and chief magistrate of Vienna, is a self-righteous martinet, determined to apply the strict letter of the law, closing his mind to any mitigating circumstances. In that mood he condemns Claudio to death for committing adultery, even though it was with his own fiancée. Escalus asks Angelo 'Whether you had not, some time in your life, erred in this point which now you censure him.' But he is implacable, until Claudio's sister, Isabella, pleads with him. Then his rigid holier-than-thou morality collapses, as he proposes to pardon Claudio in return for satisfying his lust with Isabella: 'Yielding up thy body to my will.' His spurious rectitude is exposed as a sham, and deserves no mercy, but Isabella, the novice-nun, shows her magnanimity by forgiving him. Shakespeare, in this play, with its array of flawed characters, shows a non-judgemental understanding of human frailty: 'They say best men are moulded out of faults.'

Hypocrisy receives its strongest condemnation in King Lear, when the king "not in his perfect mind" nevertheless begins to see the hollow sham that is typical of much human behaviour:

> A man may see how this world goes with no eyes... see how yond justice rails upon yon simple thief. Hark, in thine ear: change places; and, handy-dandy, which is the justice, which is the thief? . .
> Thou rascal beadle, hold thy bloody hand!
> Why dost thou lash that whore? Strip thine own back;
> Thou hotly lusts to use her in that kind
> For which thou whipst her. The usurer hangs the cozener.   (cheat)
> Through tattered clothes small vices do appear;
> Robes and furred gowns hide all. Plate sin with gold,
> And the strong lance of justice hurtless breaks;
> Arm it in rags, a pigmy's straw doth pierce it.   (4.6.154)

- -

To round off these comments on hypocrisy, here is Hamlet once more:

> O villain, villain, smiling damnèd villain!
> My tables – meet it is I set it down   (tablet, note-book)
> That one may smile, and smile, and be a villain.   (1.5.106)

- -

But enough of the negative – let us return to considering the positive virtues of the whole man, and among these is *generosity*. Here, Edmund Mortimer, Earl of March, gives a character sketch of his father-in-law, Owen Glendower:

> In faith, he is a worthy gentleman,
> Exceedingly well –read, and profited
> In strange concealments, valiant as a lion   (=secret arts)
> And wondrous affable, and as bountiful
> As mines of India.   (1 Hy IV 3.1.164)

How much is expressed in that last brief phrase! Such compressed thoughts and world-ranging similes demonstrate why our writer is so unique and so memorable.

Cleopatra praises the generosity of Antony:

> For his bounty,
> There was no winter in't; an autumn 'twas
> That grew the more by reaping. (5.2.86)

King Henry IV, vexed by his son's wayward behaviour, nevertheless admits that:

> He hath a tear for pity, and a hand
> Open as day for melting charity. (2 Hy IV 4.4.31)

Timon of Athens appears to be an unfinished play, as can be seen from the presence of two alternative endings, and it was never staged in Shakespeare's day as far as is known. The story comes from Plutarch, and Timon's change of mood from warm benevolence to cold malevolence was perhaps too far-fetched to inspire Shakespeare's full creative powers, and it may simply have been set aside in favour of better plays in preparation, such as Antony and Cleopatra.

> (Timon:) Imprisoned is he, say you?
> (messenger from Ventidius:)
> Ay, my good lord: five talents is his debt,
> His means most short, his creditors most strait;   (=strict)
> Your honourable letter he desires
> To those have shut him up ...
> (Timon:) Noble Ventidius! Well;
> I am not of that feather to shake off
> My friend when he must need me. I do know him
> A gentleman that well deserves a help,
> Which he shall have: I'll pay the debt and free him.
> (messenger:) Your lordship ever binds him.
> (Timon:) Commend me to him. I will send his ransom;
> And being enfranchised, bid him come to me.
> 'Tis not enough to help the feeble up,
> But to support him after. (1.1.97)

Then, despite the warnings of his faithful steward, Timon's very generosity brings him to the verge of bankruptcy. "Poor honest lord,

146

brought low by his own heart, undone by goodness." But he is confident that those who benefited from his largesse will now come to his aid, and approaches them for help, but they all refuse him, and as they "slink all away," these "most smiling, smooth, detested parasites" make their excuses:

> This is no time to lend money, especially upon
> Bare friendship, without security. (3.1.41)

(and)

> Men must learn now with pity to dispense
> For policy sits above conscience. (3.2.88)

Timon is forced to live in the woods, where he becomes misanthropic as he invokes a curse on the whole of human society:

> Piety and fear,
> Religion to the gods, peace, justice, truth,
> Domestic awe, night-rest and neighbourhood,
> Instruction, manners, mysteries and trades, (mysteries=craft skills)
> Degrees, observances, customs and laws,
> Decline to your confounding contraries ... (4.1.15)

(see note about Timon at the end of the chapter.)

The student of human nature keeps returning to Hamlet:

> (Hamlet:) Good my lord, will you see the players well bestowed? Do you hear, let them be well used, for they are the abstracts and brief chronicles of the time; after your death you were better have a bad epitaph than their ill report while you live.
> (Polonius:) My lord, I will use them according to their desert.
> (Hamlet:) God's bodikins, man, much better! Use every man after his desert, and who should 'scape whipping? Use them after your own honour and dignity: the less they deserve, the more merit is in your bounty. (2.2.518)

The antithesis of an open and generous nature is the closed mind unable to empathise with others. Such people cannot or will not reciprocate kindnesses, and this *ingratitude* is condemned by our author in several passages. First, Viola in Twelfth Night:

> I hate ingratitude more in a man
> Than lying, vainness, babbling, drunkenness

147

Or any taint of vice whose strong corruption
Inhabits our frail blood.   (TN 3.4.166)

And we have already heard Amiens sing, in As You Like It:
    Blow, blow, thou winter wind,
    Thou art not so unkind
    As man's ingratitude.   (AYLI 2.7.174)
    King Lear cannot believe that his daughters, his own flesh and blood,
have rejected him:
    How sharper than a serpent's tooth it is
    To have a thankless child.   (KL 1.4.295)
And when they turn him out into the storm:
            In such a night
    To shut me out! …
            … O Regan, Goneril!
    Your old kind father, whose frank heart gave all-
    O! that way madness lies; let me shun that.   (3.4.18)

Here is Lear once more, at the height of the storm:
    And thou, all -shaking thunder,
    Strike flat the thick rotundity o' the world
    Crack nature's moulds, all germens spill at once (g=the seeds of life)
    That make ingrateful man!   (KL 3.2.6)

We come now to another essential virtue of the noble mind, namely
mercy, and its near neighbours, forgiveness and compassion. In The Merchant of Venice, Portia makes the famous appeal for mercy, an appeal the
more persuasive because of the richness of the poetry:
    (Portia:) Then must the Jew be merciful.
    (Shylock:) On what compulsion must I? tell me that.
    (Portia:) The quality of mercy is not strained;
    It droppeth as the gentle rain from heaven
    Upon the place beneath: it is twice blessed;
    It blesseth him that gives and him that takes:
    'Tis mightiest in the mightiest; it becomes   (b=suits)
    The thronèd monarch better than his crown;
    His sceptre shows the force of temporal power,
    The attribute to awe and majesty,

Wherein doth sit the dread and fear of kings;
But mercy is above this sceptred sway,
It is enthronèd in the heart of kings,
It is an attribute to God himself;
And earthly power doth then show likest God's
When mercy seasons justice. Therefore, Jew,
Though justice be thy plea consider this –
That in the course of justice none of us
Should see salvation: we do pray for mercy,
And that same prayer doth teach us all to render
The deeds of mercy.   (4.1.182)

When Shylock's demand for the pound of flesh turns out to make him guilty of attempted murder, a charge which carries the death penalty, the tables are turned, and Portia says:
Down therefore and beg mercy of the duke...
And the duke intervenes:
That thou shalt see the difference of our spirits,
I pardon thee thy life before thou ask it.
For half thy wealth, it is Antonio's;
The other half comes to the general state. ...

To which Shylock bitterly responds:
Nay, take my life and all; pardon not that:
You take my house when you do take the prop
That doth sustain my house; you take my life
When you do take the means whereby I live.
(Portia:) What mercy can you render him, Antonio?
(Gratiano:) A halter gratis; nothing else, for God's sake!
(Antonio:) So please my lord the duke, and all the court,
To quit the fine for one half of his goods,
I am content; so he will let me have
The other half in use, to render it,
Upon his death, unto the gentleman
That lately stole his daughter.   (4.1.364)

An important side issue here is the strong whiff of antisemitism, and it needs to be tackled, before we move on with our main themes. Is our

149

universal man somewhat less than universal? Probably, and he deserves censure for it. However, there are some comments to be made in mitigation. Firstly it is unlikely in the extreme that Shakespeare, or for that matter any member of his audience, had ever consciously set eyes on a Jew. They had all been expelled from England three centuries earlier, and none was allowed to enter the country again until 1656. A tiny few lived here unobtrusively as nominal Christians. So Shakespeare is making fun of a semi-mythical figure as insubstantial as Count Dracula or Father Christmas. Secondly the greatest speech in Shakespeare claiming the equal rights of all men, whether Jew or Gentile, is put into the mouth of Shylock. Here he complains about Antonio:

> He hath disgraced me, and hindered me half a million, laughed at my losses, mocked at my gains, scorned my nation, thwarted my bargains, cooled my friends, heated mine enemies; and what's his reason? I am a Jew. Hath not a Jew eyes? hath not a Jew hands, organs, dimensions, senses, affections, passions? fed with the same food, hurt with the same weapons, subject to the same diseases, healed by the same means, warmed and cooled by the same winter and summer, as a Christian is? If you prick us, do we not bleed? if you tickle us, do we not laugh? if you poison us, do we not die? and if you wrong us, shall we not revenge? If we are like you in the rest, we will resemble you in that. (3.3.58)

We dislike Shylock because he is an unpleasant character, and yet we warm to his daughter Jessica because she is an attractive character, even though both are equally Jewish. For these reason I suggest that the charge of antisemitism lacks substance, and largely disappears under scrutiny.

Even with his villains, Shakespeare has a habit of giving us brief glimpses of their common humanity, and in the case of Shylock we are given a little detail which arouses our pity for the man:

> (Tubal:) One of them showed me a ring that he had of your daughter for a monkey.
> (Shylock:) Out upon her! Thou torturest me, Tubal; it was my turquoise; I had it of Leah when I was a bachelor: I would not have given it for a wilderness of monkeys. (3.1.126)

The question as to whether Shakespeare was prejudiced against other races, and against foreigners entering the land, may be answered by quoting from that remarkable British Library manuscript we have already mentioned, the Book of Sir Thomas More, an unpublished play written by several authors in the 1590s, dealing with the events of Evil May Day 1517, when the London mob rioted in protest against the presence in the city of Lombard traders.

The issue of immigration became a source of murmuring in 1586, when a slump in trade encouraged narrow minds to rail against incomers, mainly French, Flemings and Dutch. Parliament considered a bill to expel 'alien strangers', but one Sir John Wolley had the courage and common sense to point out that 'this bill would be ill for London, for the riches and renown of the City cometh by entertaining of strangers'. That soul of chivalry, Sir Walter Raleigh, was in the opposite camp: 'whereas it is presented that for strangers it is against charity, against honour, against profit to expel them, in my opinion it is no matter of charity to relieve them.'

As we have pointed out, the three manuscript pages of the play which deal with the Evil May Day riot are thought to be in Shakespeare's own handwriting, and the command of language, the ranging imagination and the mood of compassion could hardly come from the pen of any other writer. The author, via More, appeals to the better nature of the rioters:

> You'll put down strangers,
> Kill them, cut their throats, possess their houses...
> ... Imagine that you see the wretched strangers,
> Their babies at their backs, and their poor luggage
> Plodding to th' ports and coasts for transportation ...
> ...   Say now th' king
> (As he is clement, if the offender mourn)
> Should so much come too short of your great trespass
> As but to banish you, whither would you go?
> What country, by the nature of your error,
> Should give you harbour? Go you to France or Flanders,
> To any German province, Spain or Portugal,
> Nay, anywhere that not adheres to England, -
> Why, you must needs be strangers. Would you be pleased
> To find a nation of such barbarous temper,
> That, breaking out in hideous violence,
> Would not afford you an abode on earth,

(pity; compassion)

Whet their detested knives against your throats,
Spurn you like dogs ...
                    ... what would you think
To be thus used? This is the strangers' case,
And this your mountainish inhumanity.
To which the Londoners reply:
Faith, a says true: let's do as we may be done by.

The whole tenure of that passage brings us back to our theme of
pity and **compassion**, most memorably highlighted in King Lear. As
the old king suffers the torments of rejection and guilt, and descends
into madness,*[*] his anger melts away, and he begins to see the truth
about himself and the world. Even as, exposed in the storm, he seems
to be the wreck of his former royal self, his cleansed spirit attains true
nobility, beginning in this passage to put the welfare of others before
his own:

(the scene is a part of the heath with a hovel, as the storm rages)
(Kent:) Here is the place, my lord; good my lord, enter:
The tyranny of the open night's too rough
For nature to endure.
(Lear:)   Let me alone.
(Kent:) Good my lord, enter here.
(Lear:) Prithee, go in thyself; seek thine own ease:
This tempest will not give me leave to ponder
On things would hurt me more. - But I'll go in.
(to the Fool:) In, boy; go first. - You houseless poverty –
Nay, get thee in. I'll pray, and then I'll sleep.
(the Fool goes in)
Poor naked wretches, wheresoe'er you are,
That bide the pelting of this pitiless storm,
How shall your houseless heads and unfed sides,
Your looped and windowed raggedness, defend you
From seasons such as these? O! I have ta'en
Too little care of this! Take physic, pomp;
Expose thyself to feel what wretches feel,
That thou mayst shake the superflux to them,
And show the heavens more just.   (3.4.1)

---

*   see note, end of chapter
152

(pity; mercy)

To my mind this is one of the most moving passages to be found anywhere in the plays. The spirit of it is matched by some words of the blinded Gloucester, in that same play, as he takes pity on 'Poor mad Tom', who is actually his son Edgar in disguise:

> Here, take this purse, thou whom heavens' plagues
> Have humbled to all strokes: that I am wretched
> Makes thee the happier: heavens, deal so still!
> Let the superfluous and lust -dieted man,
> That slaves your ordinance, that will not see,
> Because he doth not feel, feel your power quickly;
> So distribution should undo excess,
> And each man have enough.   (4.1.65)

'Humbled to all strokes' – brought so low as to suffer all strokes.
'Slaves your ordinance' – flouts the ordinances of heaven.
In Measure for Measure, Isabella appeals to the implacable Angelo to spare her brother's life:

> (Isabella:) Must he needs die?
> (Angelo:)   Maiden, no remedy.
> (Isabella:) Yes; I do think that you might pardon him,
> And neither heaven nor man grieve at the mercy.
> (Angelo:) I will not do't …
> (Isabella:) No ceremony that to great ones 'longs,
> Not the king's crown nor the deputed sword,
> The marshal's truncheon, nor the judge's robe,
> Become them with one half so good a grace
> As mercy does …
> (Angelo:) Your brother is a forfeit of the law,
> And you but waste your words.
> (Isabella:)   Alas! alas!
> Why, all the souls that were, were forfeit once:
> And He that might the vantage best have took
> Found out the remedy. How would you be
> If He, which is the top of judgment, should
> But judge you as you are? O, think on that;
> And mercy then will breathe within your lips,
> Like man new made.
> (Angelo:)   Be you content, fair maid;

153

It is the law, not I, condemns your brother:
Were he my kinsman, brother, or my son,
It should be thus with him; - he must die tomorrow.
… (Isabella:) Go to your bosom;
Knock there, and ask your heart what it doth know,
That's like my brother's fault. If it confess
A natural guiltiness, such as is his,
Let it not sound a thought upon your tongue
Against my brother's life. (2.2.48)

The reference to the 'remedy' is the Christian doctrine of the Redemption.

In King John, Hubert de Burgh has been ordered by the king to put out the eyes of the king's nephew, young Prince Arthur, using hot irons. The boy pleads for mercy:

Must you with hot irons burn out both mine eyes?
(Hub) Young boy, I must.
(Arth) And will you?
(Hub) And I will.
(Arth) Have you the heart? When your head did but ache,
I knit my handkercher about your brows –
The best I had, a princess wrought it me –
And I never did ask it you again;
And with my hand at midnight held your head,
And like the watchful minutes to the hour,
Still and anon cheered up the heavy time,
Saying, 'What lack you?' and 'Where lies your grief?'
Or, 'What good love may I perform for you?'
… Will you put out mine eyes?
These eyes that never did nor never shall
So much as frown on you? …
Ah! none but in this iron age would do it! …
Are you more stubborn-hard than hammered iron?
An if an angel should have come to me
And told me Hubert should put out mine eyes,
I would not have believed him.

The appeal finally reaches Hubert's conscience:
Well, see to live; I will not touch thine eyes …

154

And, pretty child, sleep doubtless and secure,
That Hubert for the wealth of all the world
Will not offend thee.   (4.1.38)

In Henry VI, Part 2, after the death of Cardinal Beaufort, the Earl of Warwick says: "So bad a death argues a monstrous life" to which the King replies: "Forbear to judge, for we are sinners all." (2 HyVI 3.3.30)

The question of mercy is the turning point in Coriolanus. Although Caius Marcius, later called Coriolanus, was a towering personality, a valiant warrior and an incorruptible servant of the state, he cannot be deemed to be a noble soul, a whole man because of his great faults of pride, haughtiness, obstinacy and, finally, desire for vengeance against his native city of Rome. Lines from the play throw light on his character: 'he hath faults, with surplus, to tire in repetition'; 'was ever man so proud as is this Marcius?'; 'you have not indeed loved the common people', the latter being, in his scornful opinion 'the many-headed multitude' and 'the mutable, rank-scented many'. Banished from Rome ('there is a world elsewhere'), he returns with an army, determined to destroy the city. At that moment of crisis, his mother Volumnia makes her moving plea for mercy, and this is the greatest test of his character.

(Volumnia:) If it were so, that our request did tend
To save the Romans, thereby to destroy
The Volsces whom you serve, you might condemn us,
As poisonous of your honour: no, our suit
Is, that you reconcile them: while the Volsces
May say, 'This mercy we have showed', the Romans,
'This we received'; and each in either side
Give the all-hail to thee, and cry, 'Be blessed
For making up this peace!' Thou know'st, great son,
The end of war's uncertain; but this is certain,
That, if thou conquer Rome, the benefit
Which thou shalt thereby reap is such a name
Whose repetition will be dogged with curses,
Whose chronicle thus writ: 'The man was noble,
But with his last attempt he wiped it out,
Destroyed his country, and his name remains
To the ensuing age abhorred,' Speak to me, son! ...
                    ... Why dost not speak?

(mercy; forgiveness, conscience)

> Think'st thou it honourable for a noble man
> Still to remember wrongs? (5.3.132)

And so her plea continues, until finally the mother, wife and child all kneel before him.

> (Coriolanus, holding Volumnia by the hand:)
> O, mother, mother!
> What have you done? ...
> O my mother! mother! O!
> You have won a happy victory to Rome;
> But, for your son, believe it, O! believe it,
> Most dangerously you have with him prevailed,
> If not most mortal to him. But let it come. (5.3.183)

It is worth a brief digression here to consider Shakespeare's source for the play. That he closely followed the narrative history in North's translation of Plutarch is clear when one finds many parallels of vocabulary and phrase, such as the following in North:

> So, though the ende of warre be uncertaine, yet this notwithstanding is most certaine: that if it be thy chaunce to conquer, this benefit shalt thou reape of thy goodly conquest, to be chronicled the plague and destroyer of thy countrie ...
> ... he held his peace a pretty while, and aunswered not a worde. Hereupon she beganne againe to speake unto him, and sayed, 'My sonne, why doest thou not aunswer me? ... doest thou take it honorable for a noble man, to remember the wronges and injuries done him?

Here is another close parallel in her speech:

> (North:) 'thou hast not hitherto shewed thy poore mother any curtesie'
> (Shakespeare:) Thou hast never in thy life
> Showed thy dear mother any courtesy ... (5.3.160)

We get here a fascinating glimpse of Shakespeare's method of working: with North's Plutarch open before him, he writes, probably at great speed, lifting words and even whole sentences as he goes along, but turns them into sonorous poetry.

156

The contemplation of mercy leads us on to *forgiveness*, a significant theme in many of the plays, especially the later ones. This is not to say that Shakespeare ignored or glossed over the dark and evil forces in the human soul, for they provide the material out of which the tragedies are constructed. King Lear is horrified by the cruelty of his daughter: "let them anatomize Regan, see what breeds about her heart. Is there any cause in nature makes these hard hearts?" (3.6.80)

But the very depravity of human behaviour makes forgiveness such a supreme virtue. In Shakespeare it is often (but not always) conditional on repentance or remorse, and that in turn assumes a spark of *conscience* working in the recesses of the mind. Before Macbeth descends into the hell of his own making, he reveals a sense of guilt which makes him a credible human being. The witches foretold that Banquo would father a race of kings, not Macbeth:

> They hailed him father to a line of kings:
> Upon my head they placed a fruitless crown,
> And put a barren sceptre in my gripe,
> Thence to be wrench'd with an unlineal hand,
> No son of mine succeeding. If't be so,
> For Banquo's issue I have filed my mind;   (=defiled)
> For them the gracious Duncan have I murdered;
> Put rancours in the vessel of my peace
> Only for them; and mine eternal jewel
> Given to the common enemy of man,   (=Satan)
> To make them kings, the seed of Banquo kings!   (3.1.60)

His guilt continues to prick him "In the affliction of these terrible dreams that shake us nightly" and he suffers "torture of the mind".

Shakespeare portrays King Richard III as a consummate villain, but even he has a deeply troubled conscience:

> (Richard starts, coming out of his dream:)
> Have mercy, Jesu! – Soft! I did but dream –
> O coward conscience, how dost thou afflict me!
>   ... ...
> Alack, I love myself. Wherefore? for any good
> That I myself have done unto myself?
> O, no! alas, I rather hate myself

For hateful deeds committed by myself!
I am a villain: yet I lie, I am not!
Fool, of thyself speak well! - fool, do not flatter.
My conscience hath a thousand several tongues,
And every tongue brings in a several tale,
And every tale condemns me for a villain.
Perjury, perjury, in the highest degree;
Murder, stern murder, in the direst degree;
All several sins, all used in each degree,
Throng to the bar, crying all, Guilty! guilty!
I shall despair. There is no creature loves me;
And if I die no soul shall pity me:
Nay, wherefore should they, - since that I myself
Find in myself no pity to myself? (5.3.179)

In that same play Shakespeare takes a wry look at conscience as it causes the murderers of the Duke of Clarence to hesitate before committing the deed:

(First Murderer:) I thought thou hadst been resolute.
(Second Murderer:) So I am, to let him live.
(First M:) I'll back to the Duke of Gloucester, and tell him so.
(Sec. M:) Nay, I prithee, stay a little: I hope my holy humour will change; it was wont to hold me but while one tells twenty.
(First M:) How dost thou feel thyself now?
(Sec. M:) Some certain dregs of conscience are yet within me.
(First M:) Remember our reward when the deed's done.
(Sec. M:) 'Zounds! he dies! I had forgot the reward.
(First M:) Where's thy conscience now?
(Sec. M:) In the Duke of Gloucester's purse.
(First M:) So when he opens his purse to give us our reward, thy conscience flies out?
(Sec.M:) 'Tis no matter; let it go: there's few or none will entertain it. (=receive it)
(First M:) What if it come to thee again?
(Sec.M:) I'll not meddle with it; it makes a man a coward; a man cannot steal, but it accuseth him; a man cannot swear, but it checks him,; a man cannot lie with his neighbour's wife, but it detects him; 'tis a blushing shamefaced spirit, that mutinies in a

man's bosom; it fills one full of obstacles; it made me once restore
a purse of gold that by chance I found; it beggars any man that
keeps it; it is turned out of all towns and cities for a dangerous
thing; and every man that means to live well, endeavours to trust
to himself and live without it.
(First M:) 'Zounds! it is even now at my elbow, persuading me
not to kill the duke.   (1.4.116)

Only Shakespeare dares to bring humour into such a grim event, and
only he has the skill to do it and get away with it.

Did Lady Macbeth, that she-wolf, have any spark of conscience?
While her husband is in the act of murdering Duncan, her flinty mask of
self-control slips for one revealing instant:

I laid their daggers ready:
He could not miss them. Had he not resembled
My father as he slept I had done't.   (2.2.13)

However we may be repelled by her demonic nature, that glimpse
has made her a credible human being. But the mask is soon restored, and
she tries to brazen it out: "what's done is done"; "the sleeping and the
dead are but as pictures"; "a little water clears us of this deed; How easy
is it, then!" She chides Macbeth for his "infirmity of purpose" tells him
to "consider it not so deeply," and says

These deeds must not be thought
After these ways; so, it will make us make us mad.

A revealing phrase as things turn out. Lady Macbeth disappears
from the play's events for several scenes. When we see her next she is
indeed out of her mind, walking in her sleep, talking to herself and going
through the motions of washing her hands. Now she moans "will these
hands ne'er be clean?" and "all the perfumes of Arabia will not sweeten
this little hand". Her former outward confidence has gone: "what's done
is done" changes to "what's done cannot be undone."

The doctor complains sadly that "This disease is beyond my practice"
and goes on:

infected minds
To their deaf pillows will discharge their secrets;
More needs she the divine than the physician.

In a later scene Macbeth asks the doctor
How does your patient, doctor?
(Doctor:)   Not so sick, my lord,
As she is troubled with thick-coming fancies,
That keep her from her rest.
(Macbeth:)   Cure her of that:
Canst thou not minister to a mind diseased,
Pluck from the memory a rooted sorrow,
Raze out the written troubles of the brain,
And with some sweet oblivious antidote
Cleanse the stuffed bosom of that perilous stuff
Which weighs upon the heart?   (5.1.47)

Three hundred years before Freud, Shakespeare here portrays the symptoms of what modern jargon would call repression, the attempt to bury distasteful ideas in the unconscious mind, ideas which inevitably resurface in a new guise. The process is like an attempt to plug a leaking water pipe: the liquid bursts out again via some other aperture.

The preceding paragraphs have looked at conscience and the guilt that it exposes, and it is time to return to a consideration of forgiveness, with examples from the plays. First, from the comedy All's Well That Ends Well, where the King of France forgives the follies committed by his ward Bertram. Here Bertram's mother, the Countess of Rousillon, pleads for forgiveness:

'Tis past, my liege;
And I beseech your majesty to make it
Natural rebellion, done I' the blaze of youth ...
(King:)   ... My honoured lady,
I have forgiven and forgotten all,
Though my revenges were high bent upon him ...
         ... call him hither;
We are reconciled, and the first view shall kill
All repetition. Let him not ask our pardon:
The nature of his great offence is dead,
And deeper than oblivion we do bury
The incensing relics of it ...
        (enter Bertram)
(King:) I am not a day of season,

For thou mayst see a sunshine and a hail
In me at once; but to the brightest beams
Distracted clouds give way: so stand thou forth
The time is fair again.
(Bertram:)   My high-repented blames,
Dear sovereign, pardon to me.
(King:)   All is whole;
Not one word more of the consumèd time.
Let's take the instant by the forward top,
For we are old, and on our quick'st decrees
The inaudible and noiseless foot of time
Steals ere we can effect them.   (5.3.4)

This is a light-hearted moment in comedy. In the late plays, where greater wrongs have been committed, the act of forgiveness is all the nobler. In the Tempest, chance brings the usurper, Antonio, into the power of his wronged brother, Prospero, the rightful Duke of Milan. Of course, Prospero's island is a magical place, and he and Ariel exercise supernatural powers, but the play should not be dismissed as a fantasy, but should be seen as an allegory of the real world and what goes on there. For the purposes of his story, Shakespeare has created a simplified state, a miniature world, like the Garden of Eden perhaps, with the inhabitants pared down to a few human actors, each with the freewill to chooses good or evil – the magical background has no influence on that.

(Prospero:)   Say, my spirit,
How fares the king and 's followers?
(Ariel:)   Confined together
In the same fallen fashion as you gave in charge:
Just as you left them, sir; all prisoners ...
... if you now beheld them, your affections
Would become tender,
(Prospero:)   Dost thou think so, spirit?
(Ariel:) Mine would, sir, were I human.
(Prospero:)   And mine shall.
Hast thou, which art but air, a touch, a feeling
Of their afflictions? and shall not myself,
One of their kind, that relish all as sharply
Passion as they, be kindlier moved than thou art?

161

(forgiveness, contrition, self-knowledge)

> Though with their high wrongs I am struck to the quick,
> Yet, with my nobler reason, 'gainst my fury
> Do I take part: the rarer action is
> In virtue than in vengeance: they being penitent,
> The sole drift of my purpose doth extend
> Not a frown further. Go, release them, Ariel;
> My charms I'll break, their senses I'll restore
> And they shall be themselves. (5.1.6)

And thus Prospero forgives, "they being penitent."

In an earlier scene, Alonso, king of Naples, lies asleep on the ground, and Antonio, who seized the Dukedom of Milan from his brother Prospero, tempts Sebastian to stab his brother Alonso and so replace him on the throne. Sebastian has doubts:

> (Seb:) But, for your conscience, -
> (Antonio:) Ay, sir; where lies that? If it were a kibe   (=blister)
> 'Twould put me to my slipper; but I feel not
> This deity in my bosom: twenty consciences
> That stand 'twixt me and Milan, candied be they
> And melt ere they molest! (2.1.283)

Antonio is finally brought face to face with his brother, but, unrepentant to the last, he does not ask for pardon, though if he had done it would have given the audience a warm glow towards the fellow. But Shakespeare is not always determined to please audiences, as we see when he allows Cordelia to be killed. In this present case he deliberately creates Antonio to be unregenerate, yet in spite of that, or even because of that, forgiveness is the right moral imperative:

> For you most wicked sir, whom to call brother
> Would even infect my mouth, I do forgive
> Thy rankest fault. (5.1.130)

Prospero's pardon extends to Caliban:

> Go, sirrah, to my cell;
>   … as you look
> To have my pardon, trim it handsomely.
> (Caliban:) Ay, that I will; and I'll be wise hereafter,
> And seek for grace. (5.1.291)

162

In Shakespeare's world, wrongs are to be forgiven, in a spirit of magnanimity. Here is another example from Cymbeline:

> (Iachimo kneels before Posthumus, whom he has wronged:)
> ... my heavy conscience sinks my knee,
>   ... Take that life, beseech you,
> Which I so often owe ... .
> (Posthumus:)   Kneel not to me:
> The power that I have on you, is to spare you:
> The malice towards you, to forgive you.   Live
> And deal with others better.   (5.5.414)

The contrition of a wrongdoer implies self-examination. In the Tempest Gonzago, 'the good old lord', says that after all their misadventures (and, by implication, wrong-doing) they have 'found themselves.' An important theme in some of the late plays, but especially in King Lear, is this idea of finding one's true self. We see flawed characters moving through suffering towards *self-knowledge*, when the hard exterior of self-satisfaction, arrogance and pride is swept away. This refining fire purging the soul reminds one of the saying in the lost gospel 'Q' quoted in Luke as "Whosoever shall seek to gain his life shall lose it: but whosoever shall lose his life shall preserve it," a text that must have been familiar to Shakespeare. Even the spirit, Ariel, points to Alonso suffering "heart-sorrow, and a clear life ensuing."

Only some passages in the inferior play Pericles are thought to be by Shakespeare, and it is not included in the First Folio, but these lines have the ring of authenticity:

> (Pericles:) Antiochus, I thank thee who hath taught
> My frail mortality to know itself.   (1.1.41)

In Richard the Second we follow the king on a similar journey from arrogance through self-pity to humility and an understanding of his true nature. In the abdication scene, after he has handed the crown over to Bolingbroke, he looks at himself in a mirror:

>   I'll read enough
> When I do see the very book indeed
> Where all my sins are writ, and that's myself.
>   (enter one with a glass.)
> Give me that glass, and therein will I read.

(self-knowledge, remorse)

> No deeper wrinkles yet? hath sorrow struck
> So many blows upon this face of mine
> And made no deeper wounds? O flattering glass,
> Like to my followers in prosperity,
> Thou dost beguile me. Was this the face
> That every day under his household roof
> Did keep ten thousand men? Was this the face
> That like the sun did make beholders wink?
> Is this the face which faced so many follies,
> That was at last out-faced by Bolingbroke?
> A brittle glory shineth in this face;
> As brittle as the glory is the face
> > (Dashes the glass against the ground.)
> For there it is, cracked in an hundred shivers.   (Rd II 4.1.273)

During the course of the play about King Henry the Eighth we witness the fortunes of Cardinal Wolsey as he travels on an inexorable path from the zenith of power towards utter humiliation. A textual note is in order here. Because the play appears to be uneven in quality, a theory was put forward* that it did not all come from Shakespeare's hand, but that some scenes were written by John Fletcher, who certainly was known to have collaborated with Shakespeare in writing The Two Noble Kinsmen, and the lost play, Cardenio. Modern critics tend to dismiss the collaboration theory, accepting at most that some scenes may have been 'touched up' by Fletcher.

When Wolsey is lording it over inferiors he is described as 'venom-mouthed', and Queen Katherine says of him:

> You sign your place and calling, in full seeming
> With meekness and humility; but your heart
> Is crammed with arrogancy, spleen, and pride.   (Hy VIII 2.4.106)

Then a document is produced exposing Wolsey's greed. The King hands this to him and demands that he resign his office.

> 'Tis the account
> Of all that world of wealth I have drawn together
> For mine own ends. Nay then, farewell.

---

*   J.Spedding: Who Wrote Shakespeare's Henry VIII? (1850)

(self-knowledge, remorse)

> ... I have touched the highest point of all my greatness;
> And from that full meridian of my glory,
> I haste now to my setting: I shall fall
> Like a bright exhalation in the evening,
> And no man see me more.   (3.2.211)

After the great lords have accused Wolsey of a list of crimes, the Duke of Norfolk bids him farewell:

> And so we'll leave you to your meditations
> How to live better.

Now the poetry suddenly rises to the heights, and we know that the author can be none other than Shakespeare. A tell-tale mark is the free use of metaphors drawn from everyday life.

> Farewell! a long farewell, to all my greatness!
> This is the state of man: today he puts forth
> The tender leaves of hopes; tomorrow blossoms,
> And bears his blushing honours thick upon him;
> The third day comes a frost, a killing frost;
> And when he thinks, good easy man, full surely
> His greatness is a-ripening, nips his root,
> And then he falls, as I do, I have ventured,
> Like little wanton boys that swim on bladders,
> This many summers in a sea of glory,
> But far beyond my depth: my high-blown pride
> At length broke under me, and now has left me,
> Weary and old with service, to the mercy
> Of a rude stream, that must for ever hide me.
> Vain pomp and glory of this world, I hate ye: (cf: line in Book of
> I feel my heart new opened. O! how wretched   Common Prayer)
> Is that poor man that hangs on princes' favours!
> There is, betwixt that smile we would aspire to,
> That sweet aspèct of princes, and their ruin,
> More pangs and fears than wars or women have;
> And when he falls, he falls like Lucifer,   (cf Isaiah xiv.12)
> Never to hope again.   (3.2.352)

When the superficial trappings of worldliness and wealth have been shed away, the humiliation brings with it an awareness of the essential things in life:

> I know myself now; and I feel within me
> A peace above all earthly dignities,
> A still and quiet conscience ...
> ... I am able now, methinks, -
> Out of a fortitude of soul I feel, -
> To endure more miseries and greater far
> Than my weak-hearted enemies dare offer. (3.2.379)

He warns his secretary, Thomas Cromwell, not to fall into the same errors, and defines the moral life, and this fits in with our search for 'the whole man.'

> Cromwell, I charge thee, fling away ambition:
> By that sin fell the angels; how can man then,
> The image of his Maker, hope to win by't?
> Love thyself last: cherish those hearts that hate thee;
> Corruption wins not more than honesty.
> Still in thy right hand carry gentle peace,
> To silence envious tongues: be just, and fear not. (3.2.441)

In passing, one may note an interesting point of style here, which helps to date the late plays, and that is the increased frequency of unaccented or 'weak' line endings, where the natural rhythm of the iambic pentameter would expect a final stressed syllable and no more. In the main passage quoted, perhaps three-quarters of the lines have 'weak' endings, such as *greatness, blossoms, surely* and so forth. In his maturity, the increasingly confident Shakespeare could dispense with strict adherence to narrow rules, knowing that sound, meaning, and a natural flow similar to everyday speech was more important.

The most affecting moment in any of the great plays is to be found in King Lear, where the old distracted king is reconciled to Cordelia, the daughter he has wronged. Here we have the themes of suffering, remorse, self-knowledge, and forgiveness all combined. What follows is a shortened version of the scene:

> (Cordelia:) He wakes; speak to him.
> (Doctor:) Madam, do you: 'tis fittest.

166

(Cordelia:) How does my royal lord? How fares your majesty?
(Lear:) You do me wrong to take me out o' the grave...
(Cordelia:) ... Sir, do you know me?
(Lear:) You are a spirit, I know; when did you die? ...
(Cordelia:) O! look upon me, sir,
And hold your hands in benediction o'er me.
No, sir, you must not kneel.
(Lear:)   Pray, do not mock me:
I am a very foolish fond old man,   (fond=doting, credulous)
Fourscore and upward, not an hour more or less;
And, to deal plainly,
I fear I am not in my perfect mind.
Methinks I should know you and know this man;
Yet I am doubtful: for I am mainly ignorant
What place this is ...
        ... Do not laugh at me;
For as I am a man, I think this lady
To be my child Cordelia.
(Cordelia:)   And so I am, I am.
(Lear:) Be your tears wet? Yes, faith. I pray, weep not:
I know you do not love me; for your sisters
Have, as I do remember, done me wrong:
You have some cause, they have not.
(Cordelia:)   No cause, no cause...
(Lear:) ... You must bear with me.
Pray you now, forget and forgive: I am old and foolish.   (4.7.42)
When we next see them they are Edmund's prisoners, but in spite of
that there is a kind of joy in Lear's speech, because he has been reunited
with his loving daughter;
(Lear:) Come, let's away to prison;
We two alone will sing like birds I' the cage:
When thou dost ask me blessing, I'll kneel down,
And ask of thee forgiveness: so we'll live,
And pray, and sing, and tell old tales, and laugh
At gilded butterflies, and hear poor rogues
Talk of court news; and we'll talk with them too.
Who loses and who wins; who's in, who's out;
And take upon's the mystery of things,

As if we were God's spies: and we'll wear out,
In a walled prison, pacts and sects of great ones
That ebb and flow by the moon.   (5.3.8)

In these last half dozen lines, how perfectly he sums up the ephemeral nature of courtiers and politicians, a volatile and transient world that is every bit as true today.

The brutal death of Cordelia has seemed to many critics, notably Dr Johnson, as an unnecessarily cruel end to a pessimistic play. In that I believe they have missed the main theme, for here we have seen portrayed the wonderful triumph of the human spirit, moving through sorrow and tribulation to redemption and reconciliation.

When we look at the leading women in Shakespeare's plays, there are several to whom we are attracted because of their nobility, strength of character, wit, or sheer goodness. A list of such admirable women would include Brutus' Portia and that other Portia of Belmont, Rosalind, Miranda, Cordelia, Paulina and Perdita in The Winter's Tale, Volumnia mother of Coriolanus, and Queen Katherine, wife of Henry VIIIth. It has been said that "the subtlety and breadth of Shakespeare's knowledge of feminine instinct cannot be overpraised." (Professor Walter Raleigh, Shakespeare, English men of Letters series) Some have suggested that there may have been something of the bisexual in his own character.

There is only room to print short extracts for the purposes of this book, and in the case of these women there is a lack of such quotations encapsulating their characters: we have to follow the action of each play to appreciate them to the full.

Viola, in Twelfth Night, deserves to have her name added to the list, and I like the testimonial from her brother Sebastian:

Thus far will I boldly publish her: she had a mind that envy could not but call fair.   (TN 2.1.29)

Henry the Eighth's Queen Katherine, pleading with him against divorce, clearly aroused the sympathy of Shakespeare, but he drew her character directly from his source, Holinshed's Chronicles.

First, here is Holinshed's narrative of the scene:

Sir … I desire you to doo me justice and right, and take some pitie upon me, for I am a poore woman, and a stranger, borne out of your dominion, having heere no indifferent counsell, & lesse assurance of freendship. Alas sir, what have I offended you, or what occasion of displeasure have I shewed you, intending thus to put me from you after this sort? I take God to my

168

judge, I have beene to you a true & humble wife, ever conform-
able to your will and pleasure ...   I loved for your sake all them
whome you loved, whether they were my freends or enimies.

Shakespeare, as he turned this into blank verse, kept close to his source:
    Sir, I desire you to do me right and justice,
    And to bestow your pity on me: for
    I am a most poor woman, and a stranger,
    Born out of your dominions: having here
    No judge indifferent, nor no more assurance
    Of equal friendship and proceeding. Alas sir,
    In what have I offended you? What cause
    Hath my behaviour given to your displeasure
    That thus you should proceed to put me off,
    And take your good grace from me? Heaven witness,
    I have been to you a true and humble wife,
    At all times to your will conformable ...
                    which of your friends
    Have I not strove to love, although I knew
    He were mine enemy?   (3.4.11)

Reading the chapter on Love, we felt pity for Valentine, one of the
Two Gentlemen of Verona, who had hopelessly lost his heart to a lady.
During the play she is immortalised in song:
    Who is Silvia? what is she,
        That all our swains commend her?
    Holy, fair, and wise is she;
        The heaven such grace did lend her,
    That she might admirèd be.
    Is she kind as she is fair?
        For beauty lives with kindness:
    Love doth to her eyes repair,
        To help him of his blindness;
    And, being helped, inhabits there.
    Then to Silvia let us sing
        That Silvia is excelling:
    She excels each mortal thing
        Upon the dull earth dwelling.
    To her let us garlands bring.   (TGV 4.2.40)

But Shakespeare's heroines are not to be dismissed as mere beautiful statues on pedestals. In The Winter's Tale, Leontes, the King of Sicilia, consumed by irrational jealousy, disowns his wife and his new-born child.

His timid and obsequious courtiers are reluctant to criticize him, and it is left to bold Paulina, friend of the queen, to face him down.

> He must be told on't, and he shall: the office
> Becomes a woman best. I'll take't upon me:
> If I prove honey-mouthed, let my tongue blister,
> And never to my red-looked anger be
> The trumpet any more. Pray you, Emilia,
> Commend my best obedience to the queen:
> If she dares trust me with her little babe,
> I'll show't the king, and undertake to be
> Her advocate to th'loud'st. We do not know
> How he may soften at the sight o'th'child:
> The silence often of pure innocence
> Persuades, when speaking fails.
> (Emilia:)   Most worthy madam,
> Your honour and your goodness is so evident,
> That your free undertaking cannot miss
> A thriving issue: there is no lady living   (issue=outcome)
> So meet for this great errand …
> (Paulina:)   … Tell her, Emilia,
> I'll use that tongue I have: if wit flow from't
> As boldness from my bosom, let't not be doubted
> I shall do good.   (2.2.31)

One of the most attractive characters in King Lear is the Duke of Kent, banished by the old king in a fit of temper, but returning, in disguise, determined to serve and protect him:

> (Lear:) What art thou?
> (Kent:) A man, sir.
> (Lear:) What dost thou profess? What wouldst thou with me?
> (Kent:) I do profess to be no less than I seem; to serve him truly
> that will put me in trust; to love him that is honest; to converse
> with him that is wise and says little; to fear judgment; to fight
> when I cannot choose; and to eat no fish.

(Lear:) What art thou?

(Kent:) A very honest-hearted fellow, and as poor as the king.

(Lear:) If thou be'st as poor for a subject as he's for a king, thou art poor enough. What wouldst thou?

(Kent:) Service

(Lear:) Who wouldst thou serve?

(Kent:) You.

(Lear:) Dost thou know me, fellow?

(Kent:) No, sir; but you have that in your countenance which I would fain call master.

(Lear:) What's that?

(Kent:) Authority.

(Lear:) What services canst thou do?

(Kent:) I can keep honest counsel, ride, run, mar a curious tale in telling it, and deliver a plain message bluntly: that which ordinary men are fit for, I am qualified in: and the best of me is diligence ...

(Lear:) ... Follow me; thou shalt serve me: if I like thee no worse after dinner, I will not part from thee yet.   (1.4.10)

_ _ _ _ _ _ _ _ _ _ _ _ _ _ _ _ _ _ _

To bring this chapter to a close, I append passages which sum up the whole man, the rounded person, the essence of the noble mind:

Hamlet is said to be -

Most generous, and free from all contriving   (4.7.135)

\- \-

And Othello has a similar character -

The Moor is of a free and open nature

That thinks men honest that but seem to be so.   (1.3.405)

When old Adam offers to act as a servant to Orlando, the latter replies:

O good old man; how well in thee appears

The constant service of the antique world,

When service sweat for duty, not for meed!   (m=reward)

Thou art not for the fashion of these times,

Where none will sweat but for promotion.   (AYLI 2.3.56)

171

- -

(Measure for Measure, the character of Duke Vincentio:)
    (Duke, disguised:) I pray you, sir, of what disposition was
    the duke?
    (Escalus:) One that, above all other strifes, contended
    Especially to know himself.
    (Duke:) What pleasure was he given to?
    (Escalus:) Rather rejoicing to see another merry ...
    ... a gentleman of all temperance. (3.2.250)

- -

(The character of Troilus:)
    (Ulysses:) ... a true knight;
    Not yet mature, yet matchless: firm of word;
    Speaking in deeds, and deedless in his tongue;
    Not soon provoked, nor, being provoked, soon calmed:
    His heart and hand both open and both free;
    For what he has he gives, what thinks, he shows;
    Yet gives he not till judgment guide his bounty,
    Nor dignifies an impure thought with breath.
    (impare in Q=unworthy)(1.2.271)

(and Pandarus chides his niece Cressida for her failure to recognize
the virtues of Troilus:)
    ... have you any discretion? have you any eyes? do you know
    what a man is? Is not birth, beauty, good shape, discourse, man-
    hood, learning, gentleness, virtue, youth, liberality, and such like,
    the spice and salt that season a man?(1.2.271)

- -

The conspirators who killed Julius Caesar have been defeated in battle, and the victor, Antony, sees the corpse of Brutus:
    This was the noblest Roman of them all:
    All the conspirators, save only he,
    Did that they did in envy of great Caesar;
    He only, in a general honest thought,
    And common good to all, made one of them.
    His life was gentle; and the elements
    So mixed in him that Nature might stand up

And say to all the world, *This was a man!*   (5.5.68)

- -

And under the heading of 'whole man' may we not find a place for William himself, based on the testimony of his friend, Ben Jonson? After referring to "My gentle Shakespeare, Sweet Swan of Avon" he goes on: "I loved the man and do honour his memory on this side idolatry as much as any. He was indeed honest, and of an open and free nature, had an excellent phantasy (fancy, imagination), brave notions, and gentle expressions."

A note on the madness of King Lear (see page 114):

The story of King Lear is found in more than forty versions in old chronicles, and before Shakespeare's play it had been put on the stage more than once, most recently in 1594. But it is remarkable that Shakespeare alone portrays the king as descending into madness. Perhaps that was suggested to him by a situation which affected a family known to his patron, the Earl of Southampton. Sir Brian Annesley, who had been a member of Queen Elizabeth's court, was described in October 1603 as "altogether unfit to govern himself or his estate". Two of his three daughters tried to have him certified as insane, in order to get their hands on his estate, but the youngest daughter wrote a letter of protest to Robert Cecil (formerly Secretary of State to Elizabeth) claiming that her father's services to the late queen "deserved a better agnomination (name) than at his last gasp to be recorded and registered a Lunatic". By a strange coincidence her name was Cordell. In 1608 she married Sir William Harvey, who was widower of the Dowager Countess of Southampton and therefore stepfather of Shakespeare's patron. In the 1594 play, the youngest daughter of 'King Leir' was called Cordella.

"HERE IS MY JOURNEY'S END" (Oth 5.2.265)

All we who breathe fresh air and walk with cheerful steps through this beautiful world try to postpone the inevitable thought that all life ends in death. "Nothing 'gainst Time's scythe can make defence."

(Son 12)

> The end crowns all,
> And that old common arbitrator, Time
> Will one day end it. (T&C 4.5.223)

In Measure For Measure, the condemned Claudio laments that:
> Death is a fearful thing ...
> ... to die, and go we know not where;
> To lie in cold obstruction and to rot;
> This sensible warm motion to become
> A kneaded clod; and the delighted spirit ...
> ... To be imprisoned in the viewless winds,
> And blown with restless violence round about
> The pendant world ...
> ... 'tis too horrible!
> The weariest and most loathèd worldly life
> That age, ache, penury and imprisonment
> Can lay on nature is a paradise
> To what we fear of death. (3.1.155)

The contrast between once-vibrant life and the horror of the decaying corpse comes as a sudden shock to Hamlet in the graveyard:
> (Gravedigger:) Here's a skull now; this skull has lain in the earth three-and twenty years.
> (Hamlet:) Whose was it?
> (Gravedigger:) A whoreson mad fellow's it was: whose do you think it was?
> (Hamlet:) Nay, I know not.
> (Gravedigger:) A pestilence on him for a mad rogue! 'a poured a flagon of Rhenish on my head once. This same skull, sir, was

Yorick's skull, the king's jester.

(Hamlet:) This?

(Gravedigger:) E'en that.

(Hamlet:) Let me see. (takes the skull) – Alas, poor Yorick! –

     - I knew him, Horatio; a fellow of infinite jest, of most excellent fancy: he hath borne me on his back a thousand times; and now, how abhorrèd in my imagination it is! my gorge rises at it. Here hung those lips that I have kissed I know not how oft. Where be your jibes now? Your gambols? Your songs? Your flashes of merriment, that were wont to set the table on a roar? Not one now, to mock your own grinning? Quite chop-fallen? Now get you to my lady's chamber, and tell her, let her paint an inch thick, to this favour she must come: make her laugh at that. Prithee, Horatio, tell me one thing.

(Horatio:) What's that, my lord?

(Hamlet:) Dost thou think Alexander looked 'o this fashion I' the earth?

(Horation:) E'en so.

(Hamlet:) And smelt so? pah!   (throws down the skull)

(Horatio:) E'en so, my lord.   (5.1.188)

                (favour=face, visage)

      (chop-fallen=down in the mouth, dejected)

In passing, the reader has to confess that he is drawn into the 'reality' of this scene. We feel we were present at this conversation, and that Yorick actually existed, and that we heard the laughter at that table.

     .. As imagination bodies forth

The forms of things unknown, the poet's pen

Turns them to shapes, and gives to airy nothing

a local habitation and a name.

Death is especially poignant when it extinguishes a young life. In 1596 Shakespeare's son Hamnet died at the age of eleven. The father's bitter sorrow is expressed in King John, written later that year. Constance bewails the loss of her son Arthur:

     Never, never

Must I behold my pretty Arthur more ...

Grief fills up the room of my absent child,

Lies in his bed, walks up and down with me,

Puts on his pretty looks, repeats his words,

Remembers me of all his gracious parts,
Stuffs out his vacant garments with his form ...
O Lord! my boy, my Arthur, my fair son!
My life, my joy, my food, my all the world!   (3.4.88)

- -

Even the death of such an old reprobate as Falstaff can arouse our
sympathy when it is described in such a vivid and convincing way:

(Pistol:) ...   Falstaff he is dead, and we must yearn therefore.

(yearn=grieve)

(Bardolph:) Would I were with him, wheresome'er he is, either
in heaven or in hell.

(Hostess:) Nay, sure, he's not in hell: he's in Arthur's bosom, if
ever man went to Arthur's bosom. A' made a finer end and went
away an it had been any christom child;* a' parted even just between twelve and one, even at the turning o' the tide; for after I
saw him fumble with the sheets and play with flowers and smile
upon his fingers' ends, I knew there was but one way; for his
nose was as sharp as a pen, and a' babbled† of green fields. 'How
now, Sir John!' quoth I: 'what man! be of good cheer.' So a' cried
out 'God, God, God!' three or four times: now I, to comfort him,
bid him a' should not think of God, I hoped there was no need
to trouble himself with any such thoughts yet. So a' bade me
lay more clothes on his feet: I put my hand into the bed and felt
them, and they were as cold as any stone; then I felt to his knees,
and so upward and upward, and all was as cold as any stone.

(Hy V 2.3.5)

In the history plays, and in the tragedies, death comes often in a violent form, to innocent and guilty alike.

(Macbeth has a cynical view of life and death:)
I have lived long enough: my way of life
Is fallen into the sear, the yellow leaf;   (s=withered)
And that which should accompany old age,
As honour, love, obedience, troops of friends,
I must not look to have; but, in their stead,

---

*   christom child – christom, cloth used at baptism, re-used as shroud for child that
dies within a month of birth.

†   a' babbled – Lewis Theobald's suggestion (1726), to make sense of 'a Table' in
Folio.

Curses, not loud but deep, mouth-honour, breath,
Which the poor heart would fain deny, and dare not.   (5.3.22)

Note that Shakespeare's villains are human still, with a heart. He envies the man he has murdered:

better be with the dead,
Whom we, to gain our peace, have sent to peace,
Than on the torture of the mind to lie
In restless ecstasy. Duncan is in his grave;   (e=state of fear, anxiety)
After life's fitful fever he sleeps well;
Treason has done his worst: nor steel, nor poison,
Malice domestic, foreign levy, nothing
Can touch him further.   (3.2.19)

The deepest emotions call forth the greatest poetry, as we see here. 'After life's fitful fever he sleeps well' – how effectively the sounds of the words express two contrasting moods in one short sentence.

Finally Macbeth descends into pessimism and nihilism, his words displaying an extraordinary range of ideas springing from the author's soaring imagination:

(Macbeth:)   Wherefore was that cry?
(Seyton:) The queen, my lord, is dead.
(Macbeth:) She should have died hereafter;
There would have been a time for such a word –
Tomorrow, and tomorrow, and tomorrow,
Creeps in this petty pace from day to day,
To the last syllable of recorded time;
And all our yesterdays have lighted fools
The way to dusty death. Out, out, brief candle!
Life's but a walking shadow; a poor player,
That struts and frets his hour upon the stage,
And then is heard no more; it is a tale
Told by an idiot, full of sound and fury,
Signifying nothing.   (5.5.15)

This mood of world-weariness afflicted Hamlet:

O, that this too too solid flesh would melt   (solid, F; sallied, Q1, Q2)
Thaw, and resolve itself into a dew!
Or that the Everlasting had not fixed
His canon 'gainst self-slaughter! O God! O God!

How weary, stale, flat, and unprofitable
Seem to me all the uses of this world!
Fie on't! O fie! 'tis an unweeded garden
That grows to seed; things rank and gross in nature
Possess it merely.   (1.2.129)

… … … … … … … … … .

I have of late, but wherefore I know not, lost all my mirth, fore-
gone all custom of exercises; and indeed it goes so heavily with
my disposition that this goodly frame, the earth, seems to me a
sterile promontory, this most excellent canopy, the air, look you,
this brave o'erhanging firmament, this majestical roof fretted with
golden fire, why, it appears no other thing to me than a foul and
pestilent congregation of vapours.   (2.2.295)

    Richard the Second, deposed from the throne, muses on the death of
kings, and Shakespeare rises to the occasion with a brilliant blending of
ideas and word-sounds:

> Of comfort no man speak.
> Let's talk of graves, of worms and epitaphs,
> Make dust our paper and with rainy eyes
> Write sorrow on the bosom of the earth.
> Let's choose executors and talk of wills –
> And yet not so. For what can we bequeath
> Save our deposèd bodies to the ground?
> Our lands, our lives, and all are Bolingbroke's,
> And that small model of the barren earth
> Which serves as paste and cover to our bones.
> For God's sake let us sit upon the ground
> And tell sad stories of the death of kings –
> How some have been deposed, some slain in war,
> Some haunted by the ghosts they have deposed.
> Some poisoned by their wives, some sleeping killed –
> All murdered. For within the hollow crown
> That rounds the mortal temples of a king
> Keeps Death his court; and there the antic sits   (=clown)
> Scoffing his state and grinning at his pomp,
> Allowing him a breath, a little scene
> To monarchise, be feared, and kill with looks,
> As if this flesh which walls about our life
> Were brass impregnable; and, humoured thus,

Comes at the last, and with a little pin
Bores through his castle wall, and – farewell king! ...
... you have but mistook me all this while.
I live with bread like you, feel want,
Taste grief, need friends. Subjected thus,
How can you say to me I am a king?   (3.2.144)

Later, Richard foresees the fate he must accept:
I'll give ...
... my large kingdom for a little grave,
a little little grave, an obscure grave;
Or I'll be buried in the King's highway,
Some way of common trade where subjects' feet
May hourly trample on their sovereign's head;
For on my heart they tread now whilst I live.   (3.3.147)

That repetition of 'little' has a natural flow to it, as in real conversation.

In Shakespeare's treatment of death we may detect a consistent philosophical attitude of brave and stoical acceptance of the inevitable, as we see in these following extracts:
(Caesar:) Cowards die many times before their deaths;
The valiant never taste of death but once.
Of all the wonders that I yet have heard,
It seems to me most strange that men should fear;
Seeing that death, a necessary end,
Will come when it will come.   (2.3.32)

In King Lear, Edgar, the disguised son of blinded Gloucester, helps him flee from the battlefield:
(Edgar:) Away, old man! give me thy hand: away!
King Lear hath lost, he and his daughter ta'en.
Give me thy hand; come on.
(Gloucester:) No further, sir; a man may rot even here.
(Edgar:) What, in ill thoughts again? Men must endure
Their going hence, even as their coming hither:
Ripeness is all.   (5.2.5)

In an earlier chapter we saw Falstaff pressing into service his rag-tag army of unlikely recruits. Some avoid service by offering a bribe, but, as we saw, Feeble declines that way out, shrugs his shoulders and accepts his fate:

> (Feeble:) By my troth, I care not; a man can die but once; We owe God a death. I'll ne'er bear a base mind: an't be my destiny, so; an't be not, so. No man's too good to serve's prince; and let it go which way it will, he that dies this year is quit for the next ... Faith, I'll bear no base mind.   (2 Hy IV 3.2.242)

The last harrowing scene in King Lear brings tears to our eyes, and yet in a strange sense is also uplifting, as we try to grapple with the final mysteries. The death of Cordelia is the ultimate anguish which hastens the end for Lear himself:

> (Lear:)   No, no, no life!
> Why should a dog, a horse, a rat, have life,
> And thou no breath at all? Thou'lt come no more,
> Never, never, never, never, never!
> Pray you, undo this button: thank you, sir.
> Do you see this? Look on her, look, her lips,
> Look there, look there!   (dies.)
> (Edgar:)   He faints! – my lord, my lord!
> (Kent:) Break, heart; I prithee, break!
> (Edgar:)   Look up, my lord.
> (Kent:) Vex not his ghost; O! let him pass; he hates him
> That would upon the rack of this tough world
> Stretch him out longer.   (KL 5.3.317)

Shakespeare had an enormous vocabulary at his command, yet was content, in this scene, to use the simplest monosyllables to convey the deepest feelings.

In the case of a violent death suffered by a noble soul, Shakespeare manages to describe it with fitting and uplifting words:

Here Brutus, on the battlefield of Philippi, knows defeat has come:

> (Brutus:) Come hither, good Volumnius: list a word.
> (Vol:) What says my lord?
> (Brutus:)   Why, this, Volumnius ...
> I know my hour is come.
> (Vol:) Not so, my lord.
> (Brutus:) Nay, I am sure it is Volumnius.
> Thou seest the world, Volumnius, how it goes:
> Our enemies have beat us to the pit   (Low alarums)

It is more worthy to leap in ourselves
Than tarry till they push us. Good Volumnius,
Thou know'st that we two went to school together: (detail from
Even for that our love of old, I pray thee,   Plutarch)
Hold thou my sword-hilts whilst I run on it.
(Vol:) That's not an office for a friend, my lord.   (Alarum still)
(Clitus:) Fly, fly, my lord: there is no tarrying here.
(Brutus:) Farewell to you – and you – and you, Volumnius …
. . . .   Countrymen,
My heart doth joy that yet, in all my life,
I found no man but he was true to me.   (more details from Plutarch)
I shall have glory by this losing day
More than Octavius and Mark Antony
By this vile conquest shall attain unto … .
… (Cli:) Fly, my lord, fly.
(Brutus:)   Hence! I will follow.
I prithee, Strato, stay thou by thy lord:
Thou art a fellow of a good respect;
Thy life hath had some smatch of honour in it:
Hold, then, my sword, and turn away thy face,
While I do run upon it. Wilt thou, Strato?
(Strato:) Give me your hand first: fare you well, my lord.
(Brutus:) Farewell, good Strato.   (runs on his sword)
Caesar, now be still:
I killed not thee with half so good a will.   (Dies.)
                                                            (5.5.15)

. . . .
(Antony:) This was the noblest Roman of them all;
All the conspirators save only he
Did that they did in envy of great Caesar;   (based on Plutarch)
He only, in general honest thought
And common good to all, made one of them.
His life was gentle, and the elements
So mixed in him that Nature might stand up
And say to all the world, 'This was a man!'   (5.5.68)
- -

Suicide is never to be recommended, but the death of Cleopatra by
her own hand is described by Shakespeare in the noblest language, which
owes nothing to his source, North's Plutarch. Her motive was to avoid

the humiliation of being captured and forced to walk in chains through the streets of Rome, where

> (Cleo:)   … mechanic slaves
> With greasy aprons, rules, and hammers shall
> Uplift us to the view. In their thick breaths,
> Rank of gross diet, shall we be enclouded,
> And forced to drink their vapour.
> (Iras:)   The gods forbid!
> (Cleo:) Nay, 'tis most certain, Iras, saucy lictors   (lictors=officials
> Will catch at us like strumpets, and scald rhymers   who policed
> Ballad us out o' tune.   the streets)

And so, calmly, she prepares for death
(what follows is an abbreviation)

> Give me my robe, put on my crown, I have
> Immortal longings in me …   (she holds the asp to her breast)
> … Come thou mortal wretch
> With thy sharp teeth this knot intrinsicate   (=intricate)
> Of life at once untie. Poor venomous fool
> Be angry, and dispatch …   (Then death comes -)
> As sweet as balm, as soft as air, as gentle.

- -

(Her lady in waiting, Charmian, is given the final immortal lines:)

> So fare thee well.
> Now boast thee, death, in thy possession lies
> A lass unparalleled …   (5.2.209)

- -

On the battlefield of Shrewsbury, Henry Percy, nicknamed Hotspur, is mortally wounded by Harry, Prince of Wales:

> (Hotspur:) O, Harry! Thou hast robbed me of my youth …
> … And time, that takes survey of all the world,
> Must have a stop. O! I could prophesy,
> But that the earthy and cold hand of death
> Lies on my tongue. No, Percy, thou art dust,
> And food for -   (dies)
> (Prince:)- For worms, brave Percy, Fare thee well, great heart!
> Ill-weaved ambition, how much art thou shrunk!
> When that this body did contain a spirit,
> A kingdom for it was too small a bound;

But now two paces of the vilest earth
Is room enough: this earth that bears thee dead
Bears not alive so stout a gentleman   (1 Hy IV 5.4.83)

But we have had enough of gloom. The doddering justices in Henry IV, Part 2, look back on lusty student days at the Inns of Court, and consider how many acquaintances are dying off:

(Shallow:) Come on, come on, come on, sir; give me your hand sir, give me your hand sir; an early riser, by the rood. And how doth my good cousin Silence?

(Silence:) Good morrow, good cousin Shallow …

(Shallow:) … I dare say my cousin William is become a good scholar. He is at Oxford still, is he not?

(Silence:) Indeed, sir, to my cost.

(Shallow:) A' must, then, to the inns o' court shortly. I was once of Clement's Inn; where I think they will talk of mad Shallow yet.

(Silence:) You were called 'lusty Shallow' then, cousin.

(Shallow:) By the mass, I was called any thing; and I would have done any thing indeed too … I may say to you, we knew where the bona-robas were, and had the best of them all at commandment …

… Jesu! Jesu! the mad days that I have spent; and to see how many of mine old acquaintance are dead!

(Silence:) We shall all follow, cousin.

(Shallow:) Certain, 'tis certain; very sure, very sure: death, as the Psalmist* saith, is certain to all; all shall die …   … Death is certain. Is old Double of your town living yet?

(Silence:) Dead, sir.

(Shallow:) Jesu! Jesu! dead! a' drew a good bow; and dead! John a Gaunt loved him well, and betted much money on his head. Dead!   (3.2.1)

Hamlet's villainous uncle, plotting his death, nevertheless admits that his character is "most generous and free of all contriving", so we are not surprised to find that he has a serene attitude when considering the possibility of his own death:

what should be the fear?
I do not set my life at a pin's fee.   (1.4.65)

- -

*   perhaps Psalm 89

183

To die: to sleep;
No more; and, by a sleep to say we end
The heart-ache and the thousand natural shocks
That flesh is heir to, 'tis a consummation
Devoutly to be wished.   (3.1.64)

- -

When the fencing match is arranged between Laertes and Hamlet, his
friend Horatio advises Hamlet to call it off:

(Horatio:) You will lose this wager, my lord.
(Hamlet:) I do not think so; since he went into France, I have been
in continual practice; I shall win at the odds. But thou wouldst
not think how ill all's here about my heart; but it is no matter … .
(Horatio:) … If your mind dislike anything, obey it; I will fore-
stall their repair hither, and say you are not fit.
(Hamlet:) Not a whit, we defy augury; there's a special provi-
dence in the fall of a sparrow. If it be now, 'tis not to come; if it be
not to come, it will be now; if it be not now, yet it will come: the
readiness is all.   (5.2.219)

'How ill all's here about my heart' – Shakespeare has his finger on the
pulse of real people, and can read all our deepest thoughts.

After the treacherous sword-play, when Hamlet is mortally wounded by the poisoned rapier, he attempts to tell the true story behind his
father's murder, but lacks the energy:

You that look pale and tremble at this chance,
That are but mutes or audience to this act,
Had I but time, - as this fell sergeant, death,   (fell=cruel, ruthless)
Is strict in his arrest, - O! I could tell you –
But let it be. Horatio, I am dead;
Thou liv'st; report me and my cause aright
To the unsatisfied … .
If thou didst ever hold me in thy heart,
Absent thee from felicity awhile,
And in this harsh world draw thy breath in pain,
To tell my story.   (5.2.348)

With his last breath he thinks not of himself but of the future of Denmark:

I cannot live to hear the news from England,
But I do prophesy the election lights

On Fortinbras: he has my dying voice;   (i.e. the throne)
So tell him, with the occurrents, more and less,
Which have solicited – The rest is silence.   (Dies)
(Horatio:) Now cracks a noble heart, Good night, sweet prince,
And flights of angels sing thee to thy rest!   (5.2.368)

In Cymbeline, Imogen, disguised as a young man, and seemingly
dead, is laid to rest:

        With fairest flowers
While summer lasts …
I'll sweeten thy sad grave; thou shall not lack
The flower that's like thy face, pale primrose, nor
The azured harebell, like thy veins, no, nor
The leaf of eglantine, whom not to slander,
Out-sweetened not thy breath: the ruddock   (=robin)
With charitable bill …
      … bring thee all this;
Yea, and furr'd moss besides, when flowers are none,
To winter-ground thy corse.   (4.2.218)

Then Guiderius and Arviragus recite these lines over the body:
Fear no more the heat o' the sun,
    Nor the furious winter's rages;
Thou thy worldly task hast done,
    Home art gone, and ta'en thy wages
Golden lads and girls all must,
As chimney-sweepers, come to dust.

Fear no more the frown o' the great,
    Thou art past the tyrant's stroke;
Care no more to clothe and eat;
    To thee the reed is as the oak:
The sceptre, learning, physic, must
All follow this, and come to dust.

Fear no more the lightning-flash,
    Nor the all-dreaded thunder-stone;
Fear not slander, censure rash;
    Thou hast finish'd joy and moan.
All lovers young, all lovers must

Consign to thee, and come to dust.

No exorciser harm thee!
Nor no witchcraft charm thee!
Ghost unlaid forbear thee!
Nothing ill come near thee!
Quiet consummation have;
And renownèd be thy grave!   (4.2.258)

    After the betrothal masque and dance in the Tempest, Shakespeare,
through the mouth of Prospero, bids us all farewell:
                    Be cheerful, sir:
Our revels now are ended. These our actors,
As I foretold you, were all spirits and
Are melted into air, into thin air:
And, like the baseless fabric of this vision,
The cloud-capped towers, the gorgeous palaces,
The solemn temples, the great globe itself,
Yea, all which it inherit, shall dissolve
And, like this insubstantial pageant faded,
Leave not a rack behind. We are such stuff   (rack=flying cloud)
As dreams are made on, and our little life
Is rounded with a sleep   (4.1.147)

DAILY LIFE IN SHAKESPEARE'S ENGLAND

The scenes of plays may be set in Italy, Scotland, Denmark or wherever, but from time to time there is a glimpse of daily life familiar to the author.

In Romeo and Juliet we get a convincing picture of commotion 'below stairs' as guests are being entertained in the Great Chamber:

> (Servant:) Madam, the guests are come, supper served up, you called, my young lady asked for, the nurse cursed in the pantry, and everything in extremity. I must hence to wait; I beseech you, follow straight.
>
> ....
>
> (first Servant:) Where's Potpan, that he helps not to take away?
> (presumably in scorn:) He shift a trencher! He scrape a trencher!
> (second Servant:) When good manners shall lie all in one or two men's hands, and they unwashed too, 'tis a foul thing.
> (first Servant:) Away with the joint-stools, remove the court-cupboard; look to the plate:- good thou, save me a piece of marchpane (marzipan); and as thou lovest me let the porter let in Susan Grindstone and Nell*. Antony! and Potpan!
> (second Servant:) Ay, boy, ready.
> (first Servant:) You are looked for and called for, asked for and sought for in the great chamber.
> (second Servant :) We cannot be here and there too –
> Cheerily, boys; be brisk awhile, and the longer liver take all.
>
> (1.3.100)

- -

In Henry IV, Part 2, Justice Shallow is host to Falstaff, and incidentally, gives instructions to Davy, his bailiff:

> (Shallow:) By cock and pie, sir, you shall not away tonight –
> (calls:) What, Davy, I say! ...
> (Shallow:) Davy, Davy, Davy, - let me see, Davy, let me see:-
> yes, marry, William cook, bid him come hither – Sir John, you

---

*   coming to the Servants' Ball which will follow the Main Ball.

shall not be excused ...

(Davy:) ... sir, shall we sow the headland with wheat?

(Shallow:) With red wheat, Davy. But for William cook - are there no young pigeons?

(Davy:) Yes, sir. - here is now the smith's note for shoeing and plough-irons.

(Shallow:) Let it be cast (=reckoned up) and paid.

(Davy:) Now, sir, a new link to the bucket must needs be had; - and, sir, do you mean to stop any of William's wages about the sack he lost at Hinckley fair?

(Shallow:) He shall answer it. – some pigeons, Davy, a couple of short-legged hens, a joint of mutton, and any pretty little tiny kickshaws, tell William cook.   (5.1.1)

In The Winter's Tale, Clown, the shepherd's son, uses the wool income to finance a shopping trip to buy ingredients for the forthcoming 'Sheep-shearing' feast:

Let me see – every 'leven wether tods; every tod (= 28lbs wool) yields pound and odd shilling; fifteen hundred shorn, what comes the wool to? ... I cannot do it without counters. – Let me see; what am I to buy for our sheep-shearing feast? (reads from a paper) Three pound of sugar; five pound of currants; rice – what will this sister of mine do with rice? But my father hath made her mistress of the feast, and she lays it on. She hath made me four-and-twenty nosegays for the shearers, – three-man song-men all, and very good ones; but they are most of them means (=tenors?) and basses; but one puritan amongst them, and he sings psalms to hornpipes. I must have saffron to colour the warden pies; mace; dates? – none, that's out of my note; nutmegs, seven; a race or two of ginger, - but that I may beg; four pound of prunes, and as many of raisins 'o the sun.   (warden pies were made

with pears; 'race' =root)

(4.3.32)

In Henry IV, Part 1, a couple of carriers, up at an early hour, are preparing to set out with their deliveries for that day, the scene being an inn-yard in Rochester:

(Enter a carrier, with a lantern)

188

(First Carrier:) Heigh-ho! An't be not four by the day I'll be hanged: Charles' Wain** is over the new chimney, and yet our horse not packed. What, ostler!

(Ostler, within:) Anon, anon.

(First Car:) I prithee, Tom, beat Cut's saddle, put a few flocks in the point; the poor jade is wrung in the withers out of all cess.

(enter second Carrier:) Peas and beans are as dank here as a dog, and that is the next way to give poor jades the bots: (=worms) this house is turned upside down since Robin Ostler died.

(First Car:) Poor fellow! Never joyed since the price of oats rose; it was the death of him.

(Sec. Car: I think this be the most villainous house in all London road for fleas: I am stung like a tench! by the mass, there is ne'er a king christen could be better bit than I have been since the first cock.

(Sec. Car:) Why, they will allow us ne'er a Jordan (=chamber-pot) and then we leak in the chimney; and your chamber-lie breeds fleas like a loach.   (l= fish that breeds often)

(First Car:) What, ostler! come away, and be hanged; come away!

(Second Car:) I have a gammon of bacon and two races of ginger, to be delivered as far as Charing Cross.

(First Car:) Godsbody! the turkeys in my pannier are quite starved. What, ostler! A plague on thee! hast thou never an eye in thy head? canst not hear?   (2.1.1)

Mistress Quickly, Hostess of the Boar's Head tavern in Eastcheap, goes to law to sue Falstaff for loan unpaid and breach of promise:

Thou didst swear to me upon a parcel-gilt goblet, sitting in my Dolphin chamber, at the round table, by a sea-coal fire, upon Wednesday in Wheeson (Whitsun) week, when the Prince broke thy head for liking his father to a singing-man of Windsor, thou didst swear to me then, as I was washing thy wound, to marry me and make me my lady thy wife. Canst thou deny it? Did not goodwife Keech, the butcher's wife, come in then ... to borrow a

---

* Charles' Wain is better known to us as the Plough or Seven Stars in the constellation of the Great Bear. Many new chimneys were being built at that time to cope with the change from wood burning to the more noxious coal. Shakespeare, characteristically, is concerned about the welfare of the horses.
The price of oats trebled in the three years previous to the play's first performance in 1596.

mess of vinegar, telling us she had a good dish of prawns, whereby thou didst desire to eat some, whereby I told thee they were
ill for a green wound? And didst thou not, when she was gone
downstairs, desire me to be no more so familiarity with such poor
people, saying that ere long they should call me 'Madam'? and
didst thou not kiss me, and bid me fetch thee thirty shillings? I
put thee now to thy book oath. Deny it if thou canst.

(2 Hy1V 2.1.87)

MEMORABLE PHRASES

"FAMILIAR AS HOUSEHOLD WORDS"   (Hy V 4.3.52)

Our remedies oft in ourselves do lie	AWEW 1.1.252
Poor but honest	AWEW 1.3.203
My salad days when I was green in judgment, cold in blood	A&C 1.5.73
The bright day is done, and we are for the dark	A&C 5.2.193
O, how full of briers is this working-day world!	AYLI 1.2.12
Thou art in a parlous state	AYLI 3.2.44
Well said: that was laid on with a trowel	AYLI 1.2.113
I will follow thee to the last gasp	AYLI 2.3.69
Thou speakest wiser than thou art ware of	AYLI 2.4.34
Do you not know I am a woman? When I think, I must speak	AYLI 3.2.265
An ill-favoured thing, sir, but mine own	AYLI 5.4.60
Boldness be my friend!	Cym 1.6.18
Not a mouse stirring	Ham 1.1.10
... the memory be green	Ham 1.2.2
In my mind's eye	Ham 1.2.185
A countenance more in sorrow than in anger	Ham 1.2.231
The primrose path of dalliance	Ham 1.3.50
The apparel oft proclaims the man	Ham 1.3.72
A custom more honoured in the breach than the observance	Ham 1.4.15
Something is rotten in the state of Denmark	Ham 1.4.50
There are more things in heaven and earth, Horatio, than are dreamt of in your philosophy	Ham 1.5.166
The time is out of joint	Ham 1.5.188
Though this be madness, yet there is method in't	Ham 2.2.211
I could be bounded in a nutshell, and count myself a king of infinite space	Ham 2.2.254
There is nothing either good or bad but thinking makes it so	Ham 2.2.259
'twas caviare to the general	Ham 2.2.465
... the law's delay, the insolence of office	Ham 3.1.74
The lady doth protest too much, methinks	Ham 3.2.242

These pickers and stealers (hands)	Ham 3.2.356
I will speak daggers to her, but use none	Ham 3.2.421
This is the very coinage of your brain	Ham 3.4.136
I must be cruel only to be kind	Ham 3.4.178
the enginer, hoist with his own petard	Ham 3.4.208
When sorrows come, they come not single spies, but in battalions	Ham 4.5.78
Cudgel thy brains no more about it	Ham 5.1.61
There's a divinity that shapes our ends, rough-hew them how we will	Ham 5.2.10
It did me yeoman's service	Ham 5.2.36
A towering passion	Ham 5.2.80
A hit, a very palpable hit	Ham 5.2.295
wan with care	Hy IV/1 1.1.1
Wisdom cries out in the streets and no man regards it	Hy IV 1.2.86
That's past praying for	Hy IV/1 2.4.215
I know a trick worth two of that	Hy IV/1 2.1.40
Out of this nettle, danger, we pluck the flower safety	Hy IV/1 2.1.40
Shall I not take mine ease in mine inn?	Hy IV/1 3.3.91
The better part of valour is discretion	Hy IV/1 5.4.120
Past and to come seems best; things present, worst	Hy IV/2 1.3.108
He hath eaten me out of house and home	Hy IV/2 2.1.82
Uneasy lies the head that wears a crown	Hy IV/2 3.1.31
We have heard the chimes at midnight	Hy IV/2 3.2.231
Forswear thin potations	Hy IV/2 4.3.135
Commit the oldest sins the newest kind of ways	Hy IV/2 4.5.124
We few, we happy few, we band of brothers	Hy V 4.3.60
Delays have dangerous ends	Hy VI/1 3.2.33
Love thyself last	Hy VIII 3.2.444
The common herd	JC 1.2.266
The choice and master spirits of this age	JC 3.1.163
Cry 'Havoc!' and let slip the dogs of war	JC 3.1.273
Ambition should be made of sterner stuff	JC 3.2.98
An itching palm	JC 4.3.9
How oft the sight of means to do ill deeds make ill deeds done!	KJ 4.2.219
How sharper than a serpent's tooth it is To have a thankless child	KL 1.4.312
Striving to better, oft we mar what's well	KL 1.4.371
I am a man more sinned against than sinning	KL 3.2.59

Pray you now, forget and forgive	KL 4.7.85
The wheel is come full circle	KL 5.3.176
A light heart lives long	LLL 5.2.18
When shall we three meet again, in thunder,	
lightning or in rain?	Mac 1.1.1
What! Can the devil speak true?	Mac 1.3.107
Time and the hour runs through the roughest day	Mac 1.3.146
The milk of human kindness	Mac 1.5.18
The blanket of the dark	Mac 1.5.54
The be-all and the end-all	Mac 1.7.5
Is this a dagger which I see before me,	
The handle towards my hand?	Mac 2.1.33
The primrose way to the everlasting bonfire	Mac 2.3.22
I am cabined, cribbed, confined, bound in	Mac 3.4.24
Stand not upon the order of your going, but go at once	Mac 3.4.119
I'll make assurance double sure	Mac 4.1.82
Be bloody, bold and resolute	Mac 4.2.79
I have supped full with horrors	Mac 5.5.13
I bear a charmed life	Mac 5.7.41
The miserable have no other medicine but only hope	MFM 3.1.2
The devil can cite scripture for his purpose	MoV 1.3.99
Tell me where is fancy bred, or in the heart or in the head?	MoV 3.2.63
A harmless necessary cat	MoV 4.1.55
The world's mine oyster, which I with sword will open	MWW 2.2.2
I cannot tell what the dickens his name is	MWW 3.2.16
Lord, what fools these mortals be!	MND 3.2.115
Everyone can master a grief but he that has it	MAAN 3.2.26
I will a round unvarnished tale deliver	Oth 1.3.90
The robbed that smiles steals something from the thief	Oth 1.3.208
I will wear my heart upon my sleeve for daws to peck at	Oth 1.1.64
To suckle fools and chronicle small beer	
(the lot of the domesticised wife)	Oth 2.1.157
Chaos is come again	Oth 3.3.90
I am declined into the vale of years	Oth 3.3.265
A foregone conclusion	Oth 3.3.429
One that loved not wisely, but too well	Oth 5.2.343
Eating the bitter bread of banishment	Rd II 3.1.21
O! call back yesterday, bid time return	Rd II 3.2.69
Our sea-walled garden (England)	Rd II 3.4.43
Grim necessity	Rd II 5.1.20

Now is the winter of our discontent
      Made glorious summer by this sun of York   Rd III 1.1.1
A tower of strength   Rd III 5.3.12
A horse! A horse! My kingdom for a horse!   Rd III 5.4.7
He jests at scars, that never felt a wound   R&J 2.2.1
What's in a name? That which we call a rose,
      by any other name would smell as sweet   R&J 2.2.43
Parting is such sweet sorrow   R&J 2.2.184
A plague o' both your houses!   R&J 3.1.112
There's small choice in rotten apples   TS 1.1.137
The dark backward and abysm of time   Temp 1.2.49
Misery acquaints a man with strange bedfellows   Temp 2.2.42
A born devil, on whose nature Nurture can never stick.   Temp 4.1.188
O brave new world, that has such people in it   Temp 5.1.182
The common curse of mankind, folly and ignorance   T&C 2.3.28
Wherefore are these things hid? Wherefore have these gifts a curtain
      before 'em? ... Is it a world to hide virtues in?   TN 1.3.121
I have unclasped to thee the book even of my secret soul   TN 1.4.13
She sat like Patience on a monument, smiling at grief   TN 2.4.111
Some are born great, some achieve greatness, and some
      have greatness thrust upon 'em   TN 2.5.144
You ... will laugh yourselves into stitches   TN 3.2.68
this is very midsummer madness   TN 3.4.62
More matter for a May morning   TN 3.4.148
None can be called deformed but the unkind   TN 3.4.37
A merry heart goes all the day   WT 4.2.133
Bare ruined choirs, where late the sweet birds sang   Sonnet 73
... the chronicle of wasted time   Sonnet 106
Love's not Time's fool   Sonnet 116
Love comforteth like sunshine after rain   V&A 1.799